STILL MORE
MIDDLE SCHOOL
TALKSHEETS
FOR AGES 11-14

50 CREATIVE DISCUSSIONS
FOR YOUR YOUTH GROUP

D1502037

DAVID ROGERS

 ZONDERVAN®

ZONDERVAN.com/
AUTHORTRACKER
follow your favorite authors

 youth
specialties

YOUTH SPECIALTIES

Still More Middle School Talksheets: 50 Creative Discussions for Your Youth Group
Copyright 2009 by David Rogers

Youth Specialties resources, 300 S. Pierce St., El Cajon, CA 92020 are published by Zondervan, 5300 Patterson Ave. SE, Grand Rapids, MI 49530.

ISBN 978-0-310-28493-2

Cover design by David Conn
Interior design by Brandi Etheredge Design

Printed in the United States of America

09 10 11 12 13 14 • 20 19 18 17 16 15 14 13 12 11 10 9 8 7 6 5 4 3 2 1

I am humbled that God placed me in a family tree with such deep roots and sturdy branches. You all are life to me. I thank God for you and deeply love you. Alison, Jack and Lucy: Thank you for allowing me to put on paper whatGod has put in me during my years of following Jesus while also trying to lead our family well. Mom and Dad, Sarah, Andy, Kelli, Brody and Lane, Grandmother and Granddaddy Ford, Grandmother and Granddaddy Rogers, Ernie,Mary, Leslie, Natalie and Nate, John, Mary Ellen, Katherine and Johnny, Dick, Kay, Richard, Elizabeth and Robbie, Larry and Rita, Josh, April and Ryder. Thanks also to Bob, Neil, Louie, Busby, Lightsey, Mark, Bake, Dean, Jeremy, Gary, John, Richard, Eddie, Tommy, Chris, Robbie, Crowder, J.R., Greg, Jim, Rick and Bev, Bill and Connie, Bruce and Jan, Ron, Rhodes, Burns, Toop, and Mr. Hollis: Bless you for blessing me in life, friendship, and ministry.

CONTENTS

The Hows and Whats of TalkSheets 7

1. **Call Me**—Communicating with God (Jeremiah 33:3) 13

2. **Wet Paint-Don't Touch!**—The benefits of doing life God's way (Genesis 2–3) 15

3. **Risky Business**—It's never safe or convenient to follow Jesus (Matthew 8:18-22) 17

4. **Peel Off and Chunk It**—Being a candidate for God's blessing (Proverbs 25:4, Hebrews 12:1) 19

5. **Choose Your Weapon**—Choosing to trust and worship God in life's most challenging situations (2 Chronicles 20:1-30) 21

6. **Habits**—Making corporate worship a regular part of your life (Luke 4:16; Acts 2:42, 17:2; Hebrews 10:25) 23

7. **Wishing Well**—Being honest with Jesus in the desires of your heart (John 4:4-42) 25

8. **Superhero-Superpower**—Living in the power of Christ (Ephesians 3:14-21, Colossians 1:29, Hebrews 1:1-3, James 5:16) 27

9. **Memory**—The value of knowing what God has to say about life (Genesis–Revelation; Deuteronomy 32:45-47; Psalm 119:11, 105) 29

10. **Who God Is Gonna Use**—God wants to use ordinary people to influence the lives of others (Genesis 4:21; Exodus 2:1-10, 15:19-21; Numbers 22:21-34; Judges 16:18-30; Esther 3–8; John 18:32–19:16) 31

11. **Bounce Your Eyes**—How to react when sin enters your sightline (2 Samuel 11:1-5, Job 31:1) 33

12. **Tasty!**—How tasting God's goodness affects the flavor of our lives (Psalm 34:8) 35

13. **Follow the Leader**—Being an example for other people to follow (Matthew 4:18-20, 1 Corinthians 11:1) 37

14. **The Domino Effect**—Allowing God to use you in unimaginable ways (John 6:1-13) 39

15. **I Know You**—Being known by the God who knows us completely (Jeremiah 1:4-5) 41

16. **Spitting Contest**—Determining how your life tastes in the mouth of God (Revelation 3:15-16) 43

17. **Friends: Backstabber or Front-Stabber?**—Being a true friend and sharing the hard truth (Proverbs 27:6) 45

18. **Real or Counterfeit?**—How to tell if a person is a real disciple or a counterfeit (John 8:31-32) 47

19. **Selective Hearing**—Listening for and responding to God's voice (1 Samuel 3:1-10) 49

20. **Freeze Frame**—Giving accurate pictures of Jesus by the way we live our lives (2 Corinthians 5:20) 51

21. **Open or Shut?**—Opening the door to the kingdom of God (Matthew 23:14) 53

22. **But Everybody Else Is Doing It!**—Choosing to follow God no matter what kind of peer pressure you face (Micah 4:5) 55

23. **Know-It-All**—Responding as a humble servant-leader (John 13:3-17) 57

24. **Nicknames**—Jesus gave his close friends nicknames based on the stories of their lives (Mark 3:13-19, John 13:23, Revelation 2:17) 59

25. **What's the Value?**—By becoming like Jesus, we add value to others' lives (Matthew 4:23-25; 8:1-3; 9:1-8; 9:9-13; 9:18-26; 14:13-21; 28:18-20) 61

26. **Don't Clean Your Plate**—Learning the value of saving (Proverbs 21:20) 63

27. **This Little Light of Mine**—Letting your life shine the way Jesus intended: for all the world to see (Matthew 5:14-16) 65

28. **Danger!**—Heeding God's warnings (1 Corinthians 10:7-13) 67

29. **Who's Your Daddy?**—The one relationship that truly matters is being in right standing with God (Genesis 12, 15, 17; Luke 3:7-9) 69

30. **Rebel with a Cause**—Examining Jesus' commitment to serve others (Mark 10:45) 71

31. **Free Samples**—Viewing Jesus' life and ministry as free samples of heaven and the kingdom of God (Luke 4:14-21, 31-37, 38-44) 73

32. **A Picture Is Worth a Thousand Words**—Drawing a picture of faith (Mark 2:1-5, 4:35-41, 5:21-34, 6:1-6, 10:46-52, 11:22-25, 16:14) 75

33. **The Rules of the Game**—Exploring what God expects when it comes to knowing and following the rules of life (Exodus 20:1-17) 77

34. **If You Could Take One Thing with You**—Does what we value the most match what Jesus values most? (Luke 23:32-43) 79

35. **Is Life Working for You?**—Doing the same things and expecting different results is one definition of insanity (Proverbs 26:11) 81

36. **See You Real Soon**—Exploring when Jesus will come back (Matthew 24:42-44, 25:13; Mark 13:32-37; Luke 12:40; John 14:1-3; Acts 1:10-11; 1 Thessalonians 4:16, 5:1-11; Titus 2:12-13; Hebrews 9:28; James 5:8; 2 Peter 3:10; 1 John 3:2; Revelation 1:7, 22:12, 20) 83

37. **The Fork that Changed the World**—Every decision we make could change the world for better or worse (Galatians 6:7-8) 85

38. **Beyond the Weirdness**—Looking for the meaning behind the weirdness (Isaiah 20, 55:8-9; Jeremiah 27; Ezekiel 4) 87

39. **I Assume That…**—Jesus' assumptions about his followers (Matthew 6:1-18) 89

40. **Set Apart**—Living the way God desires you to live (Psalm 4:3) 91

41. **No Saving Seats**—Being mindful of others' feelings (Luke 14:7-11) 93

42. **Every Time a Bell Rings**—Being committed to intentional prayer (James 5:16) 95

43. **Weight Problem**—What it really means to honor your parents (Exodus 20:12) 97

44. **Highs and Lows**—Looking at the elevation in our life with God (Revelation 2:5) 99

45. **Demonstrated Faith**—What does faith look like in your life? (Matthew 8:5-10) 101

46. **Medal of Honor**—God loves us for free (Isaiah 64:6) 103

47. **Procrastination?**—Trusting God's perfect timing (Philippians 1:6, 2 Peter 3:8-9) 105

48. **East and West**—Allowing God to remove your sin for good (Psalm 103:11-13, 1 John 1:8-9) 107

49. **The Cloak**—Becoming a person of contentment (Philippians 4:10-13, 1 Timothy 6:6-8, Hebrews 13:5) 109

50. **Holding It Together**—Exploring how Jesus holds our lives together (Colossians 1:15-17) 111

THE HOWS AND WHATS OF TALKSHEETS

Each of the 50 discussions includes a reproducible TalkSheet for your students to work on, as well as simple, step-by-step instructions on how to use it. All you need is this book, some Bibles, a few copies of the handouts, and some kids (some food won't hurt, either).

These TalkSheets are user-friendly and very flexible. They can be used in youth group meetings, Sunday school classes, or in Bible study groups. You can adapt them for either large or small groups. And they can be covered in only 20 minutes or explored more intensively. You can build an entire youth group meeting around a single TalkSheet, or you can use TalkSheets to supplement other materials and resources you might be covering.

LEADING A TALKSHEET DISCUSSION

TalkSheets can be used as a curriculum for your youth group, but they're designed as springboards for discussion. They encourage your kids to take part and interact with each other. And hopefully they'll do some serious thinking, discover new ideas, defend their points of view, and make decisions.

Youth today live in an active world that bombards them with the voices of society and the media—most of which drown out what they hear from the church. Youth leaders must teach the church's beliefs and values—and help young people make the right choices in a world full of options.

A TalkSheet discussion works for this very reason. While dealing with the questions and activities on the TalkSheet, your kids will think carefully about issues, compare their beliefs and values with others and with Scripture, and make their own choices. TalkSheets will challenge your group to explain and rework their ideas in a Christian atmosphere of acceptance, support, and growth.

Maybe you're asking yourself, *What will I do if the kids in my group just sit there and don't say anything?* Well, when kids don't have anything to say, a lot of times it's because they haven't had a chance or time to get their thoughts organized. Most young people haven't developed the ability to think on their feet. Since many are afraid they might sound stupid, they often avoid voicing their ideas and opinions.

The solution? TalkSheets let your kids deal with the issues in a challenging but non-threatening way before the actual discussion begins. They'll have time to organize their thoughts, write them down, and ease their fears about participating. They may even look forward to sharing their answers. Most importantly, they'll want to find out what others said and open up to talk through the topics.

If you're still a little leery about leading a discussion with your kids, that's okay. The only way to get them rolling is to get them started.

YOUR ROLE AS THE LEADER

The best discussions don't happen by accident. They require careful preparation and a sensitive, enthusiastic, and caring leader. Don't worry if you aren't experienced or don't have hours to prepare. TalkSheets are designed to help even the novice leader. The more TalkSheet discussions you lead, the easier it becomes. So keep the following tips in mind when using the TalkSheets as you get your kids talking:

BE CHOOSY

Choose a TalkSheet based on the needs and the maturity level of your group. Don't feel obligated to use the TalkSheets in the order they appear in this book. Use your best judgment and mix them up any way you want.

TRY IT YOURSELF

Once you've chosen a TalkSheet for your group, answer the questions and do the activities yourself. Though each TalkSheet session has a similar structure, they each contain different activities. Imagine your kids' reactions to the TalkSheet. This will help you prepare for the discussion and understand what you're asking them to do. Plus, you'll have some time to think of other appropriate questions, activities, and Bible verses that help tailor it to your kids.

GET SOME INSIGHT

On each leader's guide page, you'll find numerous tips and ideas for getting the most out of your discussion. You may want to add some of your own thoughts or ideas in the margins. And there's room to keep track of the date and the name of your group at the top of the leader's page. You'll also find suggestions for additional activities and discussion questions.

There are some references to Internet links throughout the TalkSheets. These are guides for you to find the resources and information you need. For additional help, be sure to visit the Youth Specialties Web site at www.YouthSpecialties.com for information on materials and other links for finding what you need. Be careful as you use the Internet and videos—you'll need to (carefully!) preview them first (if applicable, you might need to check with your supervisor if you aren't sure if they're appropriate) and try to avoid any surprises.

MAKE COPIES

Your students will need their own copies of the TalkSheet—but make sure you only make copies of the student's side of the TalkSheet. The material on the reverse side (the leader's guide) is just for you. Remember: You're permitted to make copies for your group because we've said you can—but just for your youth group…not for every youth group in your state! U.S. copyright laws haven't changed, and it's still mandatory to request permission before making copies of published material. Thank you for cooperating.

INTRODUCE THE TOPIC

It's important to have a definite starting point to your session and introduce the topic before you pass out your TalkSheets to your group. Depending on your group, keep it short and to the point. Be careful to avoid over-introducing the topic, sounding preachy, or resolving the issue before you've started. Your goal is to spark your students' interest and leave plenty of room for discussion. You may also want to tell a story, share an experience, or describe a situation or problem having to do with the topic. You might want to jump-start your group by asking something like, "What's the first thing you think of when you hear the word _____ [insert the word here]?" After a few answers, you can add something like, "Well, it seems we all have different ideas about this subject. Tonight we're going to investigate it a bit further…"

The following are excellent methods you can use to introduce any lesson in this book—
• Show a related short film or video.
• Read a passage from a book or magazine that relates to the subject.
• Play a popular song that deals with the topic.
• Perform a short skit or dramatic presentation.

- Play a simulation game or role-play, setting up the topic.
- Present current statistics, survey results, or read a newspaper article that provides recent information about the topic.
- Use posters, videos, or other visuals to help focus attention on the topic.

THE OPENER

We've designed the OPENER to be a great kick-off to the discussion. Some may work better to use before you pass out the TalkSheets. Others may work better as discussion starters after the students have completed their TalkSheets. You decide! Check out the MORE section, too—it often contains an alternate opening idea or activity that'll help get students upbeat and talking, which is perfect for leading an effective TalkSheet discussion. TIP: When you're leading a game or OPENER, consider leading it like a game-show host would. Now that may not sound very spiritual, but if you think about what a host does (builds goodwill, creates excitement, facilitates community, listens to others) that sounds pretty pastoral, doesn't it? Plus, it makes it more fun!

ALLOW ENOUGH TIME

Pass out copies of the TalkSheet to your kids after the OPENER and make sure each person has a pen or pencil and a Bible. There are usually four to six discussion activities on each TalkSheet. If your time is limited, or if you're using only a part of the Talk-Sheet, tell the group to complete only the activities you'd like them to complete.

Decide ahead of time if you'd like your students to work on the TalkSheets individually or in groups. Sometimes the TalkSheet will already have students working in small groups. Let them know how much time they have for completing the Talk-Sheet, then again when there's a minute (or so) left. Go ahead and give them some extra time and then start the discussion when everyone seems ready to go.

SET UP FOR THE DISCUSSION

Make sure the seating arrangement is inclusive and encourages a comfortable, safe atmosphere for discussion. Theater-style seating (in rows) isn't discussion-friendly. Instead, arrange the chairs in a circle or semicircle (or sit on the floor with pillows!).

SET BOUNDARIES

It'll be helpful to set a few ground rules before the discussion. Keep the rules to a minimum, of course, but let the kids know what's expected of them. Here are suggestions for some basic ground rules—

- What's said in this room stays in this room. Emphasize the importance of confidentiality. Confidentiality is vital for a good discussion. If your kids can't keep the discussion in the room, then they won't open up.
- No put-downs. Mutual respect is important. If your kids disagree with some opinions, ask them to comment on the subject (but not on the other person). It's okay to have healthy debate about different ideas, but personal attacks aren't kosher—and they detract from discussion. Communicate that your students can share their thoughts and ideas—even if they may be different or unpopular.
- There's no such thing as a dumb question. Your group members must feel free to ask questions at any time. In fact, since MORE MIDDLE SCHOOL TALKSHEETS digs into a lot of Scripture, you may get hard questions from students that you cannot immediately answer. DON'T PANIC! Affirm that it's a great question, and you aren't sure of the answer—but you'll do some study over the next week and unpack it next time (and be sure to do this).

- No one is forced to talk. Some kids will open up, some won't. Let everyone know they each have the right to pass or not answer any question.
- Only one person speaks at a time. This is a mutual respect issue. Everyone's opinion is worthwhile and deserves to be heard.

Communicate with your group that everyone needs to respect these boundaries. If you sense your group members are attacking each other or adopting a negative attitude during the discussion, stop and deal with the problem before going on. Every youth ministry needs to be a safe place where students can freely be who God created them to be without fear.

SET THE STAGE

Always phrase your questions so that you're asking for an opinion, not a be-all, end-all answer. The simple addition of the less-threatening "What do you think…" at the beginning of a question makes it a request for an opinion rather than a demand for the right answer. Your kids will relax when they feel more comfortable and confident. Plus, they'll know you actually care about their opinions, and they'll feel appreciated.

LEAD THE DISCUSSION

Discuss the TalkSheet with the group and encourage all your kids to participate. The more they contribute, the better the discussion will be.

If your youth group is big, you may divide it into smaller groups. Some of the Talksheets request that your students work in smaller groups. Once the smaller groups have completed their discussions, combine them into one large group and ask the different groups to share their ideas.

You don't have to divide the group with every TalkSheet. For some discussions you may want to vary the group size or divide the meeting into

groups of the same sex. The discussion should target the questions and answers on the TalkSheet. Go through them and ask the students to share their responses. Have them compare their answers and brainstorm new ones in addition to the ones they've written down.

AFFIRM ALL RESPONSES—RIGHT OR WRONG

Let your kids know that their comments and contributions are appreciated and important. This is especially true for those who rarely speak during group activities. Make a point of thanking them for joining in. This will be an incentive for them to participate further.

Remember that affirmation doesn't mean approval. Affirm even those comments that seem wrong to you. You'll show that everyone has a right to express ideas—no matter how controversial those ideas may be. If someone states an off-base opinion, make a mental note of the comment. Then in your wrap-up, come back to the comment or present a different point of view in a positive way. But don't reprimand the student who voiced the comment.

AVOID GIVING THE AUTHORITATIVE ANSWER

Some kids believe you have the correct answer to every question. They'll look to you for approval, even when they're answering another group member's question. If they start to focus on you for answers, redirect them toward the group by making a comment like, "Remember that you're talking to everyone, not just me."

LISTEN TO EACH PERSON

Good discussion leaders know how to listen. Although it's tempting at times, don't monopolize the discussion. Encourage others to talk first—then express your opinions during your wrap-up.

DON'T FORCE IT
Encourage all your kids to talk, but don't make them comment. Each member has the right to pass. If you feel that the discussion isn't going well, go to the next question or restate the present question to keep things moving.

DON'T TAKE SIDES
Encourage everybody to think through various positions and opinions—ask questions to get them going deeper. If everyone agrees on an issue, you can play devil's advocate with tough questions and stretch their thinking. Remain neutral—your point of view is your own, not that of the group.

DON'T LET ANYONE (INCLUDING YOU) TAKE OVER
Nearly every youth group has one person who likes to talk and is perfectly willing to express an opinion on any subject—all the time. Encourage equal participation from all members.

LET THEM LAUGH!
Discussions can be fun! Most of the TalkSheets include questions that'll make students laugh and get them thinking, too. Some of your students' answers will be hilarious—feel free to stop and laugh as a group.

LET THEM BE SILENT
Silence can be scary for discussion leaders! Some react by trying to fill the silence with a question or a comment. The following suggestions may help you to handle silence more effectively—

- Be comfortable with silence. Wait it out for 30 seconds or so to respond, which can feel like forever in a group. You may want to restate the question to give your kids a gentle nudge.
- Talk about the silence with the group. What does the silence mean? Do they really not have any comments? Maybe they're confused, embarrassed, or don't want to share.
- Answer the silence with questions or comments like, "I know this is challenging to think about..." or "It's scary to be the first to talk." If you acknowledge the silence, it may break the ice.
- Ask a different question that may be easier to handle or that'll clarify the one already posed. But don't do this too quickly without giving them time to think the first one through.
- The "two more answers" key. When you feel like moving on from a question, you may want to ask for two more answers to make sure you've heard all of the great ideas. Many students have good stuff to say, but for one reason or another choose not to share. This key skill may help you draw out some of the best answers before moving on.

KEEP IT UNDER CONTROL
Monitor the discussion. Be aware if the discussion is going in a certain direction or off track. This can happen fast, especially if your students disagree or things get heated. Mediate wisely and set the tone that you want. If your group gets bored with an issue, get them back on track. Let the discussion unfold but be sensitive to your group and who is or isn't getting involved.

If a student brings up a side issue that's interesting, decide whether or not to pursue it. If the discussion is going well and the issue is worth discussing, let them talk it through. But if things get off track, say something like, "Let's come back to that subject later if we have time. Right now, let's finish our discussion on..."

BE CREATIVE AND FLEXIBLE

If you find other ways to use the TalkSheets, use them! Go ahead and add other questions or Bible references. Don't feel pressured to spend time on every single activity. If you're short on time, you can skip some items. Stick with the questions that are the most interesting to the group.

SET YOUR GOALS

TalkSheets are designed to move along toward a goal, but you need to identify your goal in advance. What would you like your youth to learn? What truth should they discover? What's the goal of the session? If you don't know where you're going, it's doubtful you'll get there.

BE THERE FOR YOUR KIDS

Some kids may actually want to talk more with you about a certain topic. (Hey! You got 'em thinking!) Let them know you can talk one-on-one with them afterward.

CLOSE THE DISCUSSION

Present a challenge to the group by asking yourself, "What do I want my students to remember most from this discussion?" There's your wrap-up! It's important to conclude by affirming the group and offering a summary that ties the discussion together.

Sometimes you won't need a wrap-up. You may want to leave the issue hanging and discuss it in another meeting. That way, your group can think about it more and you can nail down the final ideas later.

TAKE IT FURTHER

On the leader's guide page, you'll find additional materials—labeled MORE—that provide extra assistance to you. Some sessions contain an additional activity—e.g., an opener, expanded discussion, or fun idea. Some have support material that can help you handle some potential confusion related to the topic. These aren't a must, but highly recommended. They let the kids reflect upon, evaluate, dig in a bit more, review, and assimilate what they've learned. These activities may lead to even more discussion and better learning.

1. Who were your last three text messages or phone calls to and what was said?

CALL ME

2. Circle the forms of communication you participated in this past week.
   - Face to Face
   - Email
   - Instant Message
   - Telephone
   - Cell Phone
   - Text Message
   - Sign Language
   - Written Note or Letter
   - Smoke Signals
   - Other:_____

3. Check out Jeremiah 33:3 and then finish the following phrases on your own.

   - God is suggesting that I…

   - God says that if I do, then…

   - What this tells me about God is…

   - If I decided to take God up on the offer, I'd communicate by…

4. If I were to call to God, what I'd really want to say is…

5. What I'd really love God to show me is…

THIS WEEK

Teenagers are constantly communicating with their friends via email, cell phones, text messaging, instant messaging, and talking face to face. This Talk-Sheet will get your group talking about what it looks like to communicate with God. They'll learn that God initiated communication with us through an offer in Jeremiah 33:3.

OPENER

Start by asking your students who has the quickest text-messaging skills in the group. If some students don't have a cell phone, ask them to sit near the person they believe to be the fastest and root for that student. Once the contestants have their cell phones out, ask them to text you these words: CALL TO ME AND I WILL ANSWER YOU. If you have a large group, select a few students to compete against each other, rather than have everyone text you. After the winner is named, ask how many times a day they text or call people on the phone. This will get them thinking and talking about ways they communicate. Then you can make the point that God designed people to communicate.

THE DISCUSSION, BY NUMBERS

1. Have the students jot down their answers and then spend a couple of minutes getting some feedback from them. You might ask (1) Who had the longest text or conversation? (2) Who had the shortest? (3) Who had the most random? (4) Who had the funniest? (5) Who had the most important?

2. Give the students a few minutes to think about all the forms of communication they used in the past week. Have them circle the applicable ones and write down any additional types. Call out each of the options and have students raise their hands if they circled it. If no one mentions prayer as an additional form of communication, ask them what they think about prayer and why it didn't make their list.

3. Ask a volunteer to read Jeremiah 33:3 out loud and then give the group a few minutes to finish the phrases. The point you want to make is that God desires to be in two-way communication with us. We can talk to God and expect God to answer us. He wants to hear from us and speak back into our lives about who we are, our purpose, and who God

desires us to be. Before moving on, have the group read the following passages about communication with God: Isaiah 49:8; 55:6; 65:24; Jeremiah 29:12; Daniel 9:20-23; 10:12; and 2 Corinthians 6:1-2.

4. Encourage your group to take these last two questions seriously. Remind them that God already knows what's going on inside of us (see Psalm 139:4); he just wants us to be honest about it. Let them finish both sentences before asking for their responses.

5. Ask the group to share their finished statements. Have students read both answers before moving on to someone else. Affirm their honesty as you remind them that God wants us to communicate with him.

THE CLOSE

Tell your students that God offers to be in communication with us because God desires to be in relationship with us. God speaks to us through the Bible and the trusted individuals he's placed in our lives. Oftentimes God uses the words of these people and the circumstances of our lives to answer us when we call on him. Sometimes we may hear silence. Even in those times, we must remember that God's timing is perfect. (See Ecclesiastes 3.) Answers and insights will come only in God's perfect timing. In the meantime, God desires for us to continue communicating with him through prayer. Challenge them to call on God each day and tell you how God answers them.

MORE

• **Throughout the week answer the text messages that your students sent to you at the beginning of the lesson. Encourage them to keep calling on God and listening for what God may want to share with them.**

• **Google "text message statistics" and have students guess some of the latest research about text-messaging trends.**

• **Divide the students into small groups of two or three and ask them to discuss prayer. Have them share when they pray, what they pray for, where they pray, and what they typically say when they pray. You might even suggest that they write out their prayers (journal) as a form of spiritual discipline.**

1. **If God had painted that object and put a sign beside it, what would have happened if you'd touched it and why?**

WET PAINT—
DON'T TOUCH!

2. **If you touched the object and got wet paint on your hands while God was in the other room, how would you react? I'd:**

_____ Feel afraid

_____ Run and hide

_____ Try to wash it off

_____ Blame my friend

_____ Come up with a story about how I accidentally tripped and fell into it

_____ Paint the rest of my body and hope God doesn't notice

_____ Tell God I was taking up finger painting and that was the only paint around

_____ Question God as to why and if those were really the instructions

_____ Say I'm sorry and promise never to do it again…and then cry

_____ Tell God to lighten up because it's just a little paint

_____ Say nothing and see if God notices, and then I'd play dumb: "Paint? What paint?"

_____ Just be quiet and show God the paint on my hands and the mess I made

_____ _____.

3. **Check out the first "Wet Paint" sign that God ever created in Genesis 2.**

   • Verses 8-9 tell us God did something.

   • Verses 15-17 tell us about God's "Wet Paint" sign. What do you think it was?

   • What were the consequences? Were they clear?

4. **Read Genesis 3:1-7.**

   • What did Adam and Eve decide to do?

   • Why do you think they made that choice?

   • What initially happened to them and how did they react?

5. **What does Genesis 3:8-13 tell us about how they responded next? See if any of the ways they responded are also found in question two.**

6. **Ultimately, did the consequences of God's "Wet Paint" sign come true for Adam based on the choices he made? (See Genesis 5:5.)**

THIS WEEK

Today's TalkSheet shows what happens when we choose not to do life God's way. Since the beginning, humans have struggled to believe that God's ways are best. But God keeps his word—even when we make poor choices. Because God desires the best for us, he offers guidelines that point us toward blessings and away from curses.

OPENER

Before your students arrive, find a prominent place to put a painted object, such as a block of wood. Make sure the paint is dry, but place a sign next to it that reads: WET PAINT—DON'T TOUCH…OR YOU'LL GET PAINT ON YOUR FINGERS. You're conducting an experiment (okay, it's a temptation trap) to see who touches the painted object and who chooses to follow the instructions. Bring the painted object and sign to the center of the discussion area and use it as the primary object lesson for the discussion. Ask for a show of hands as to how many touched the object and how many didn't. Choose a few students to share the reason for their choice.

THE DISCUSSION, BY NUMBERS

1. The point you want to make is that God keeps his word. If God's sign had said they'd get paint on their fingers, then it would've happened.

2. Give them a few minutes and then ask them to share their response(s). (It's okay if students have more than one answer.) If someone makes the point that God is omnipresent, agree and say they should keep that in mind with any choice they make.

3. Ask the group to turn to Genesis 2 and fill in all three parts to question three before sharing their answers. The main point is that God didn't have to create anything or anybody. God chose to do so for his own pleasure. And because God didn't desire a robot, God gave man the choice to be obedient. Adam had one clear rule to follow—he could eat the fruit from any plant except for one tree. If he ate from that tree, he'd die.

4. Ask the group to read Genesis 3:1-7 and answer question four. Adam and Eve ate the forbidden fruit and let the serpent deceive them. Be sure to look at verse 4 before moving to the next question. It's important for the students to see that what the serpent (Satan) said in verse 4 is in direct opposition to what God said in Genesis 2:17.

5. This is where they'll hopefully see that Adam and Eve's reasons resemble the ones your students gave earlier. Ask the group to read Genesis 3:8-13 and look for similarities between Adam and Eve's answers and their own responses to question two (fear, hiding, and playing the blame game).

6. Ultimately, Adam (and Eve) died. God kept his word. If your group suggests that it was a long time before that happened, point out the immediate consequences mentioned in verses 16 (painful childbirth), 17-19 (hard work), and 21-24 (God kicked them out of Eden).

THE CLOSE

God desires the very best for our lives (see Jeremiah 29:10-14 and Matthew 7:9-11). However, God also keeps his word. We choose to be blessed when we follow God's plans. But the flip side is that we choose curses when we go our own way. Read aloud Deuteronomy 30:19-20 to end your time.

MORE

• **Provide an inkpad so students can use their thumb or pointer finger to stamp their TalkSheets as a tangible sign of their commitment to obey God this week.**

• **Go back to Genesis 3:21 and make the parallel between this verse and Jesus' death. This scene can be used to talk about how God goes to extremes to cover our mistakes and bring us back into a right relationship with him. God killed an innocent animal and used its skin to cover the nakedness and shame of Adam and Eve. God sent Jesus to die so he might cover our shame and sin. (See Romans 3:23; 5:8; 6:23; 10:9-10; 10:13, and 2 Corinthians 5:14-21.)**

• **It might be interesting for your group to compare the progression from sin to death in Genesis 2–3 (especially verse 2:17) with the following passages: Job 15:35, Psalm 7:14, Isaiah 59:14, Romans 5:12, Romans 6:23, and James 1:13-15.**

1. Check out Matthew 8:18-22 and then answer the following questions:

- In verse 20 Jesus says, "Foxes have holes and birds have nests, but the Son of Man has no place to lay his head." What do you think he means by this saying?

- In verse 21 a disciple says, "Lord, first let me go and bury my father." What do you think he means?

- In verse 22 Jesus says, "Follow me, and let the dead bury their own dead." What do you think he means?

2. The riskiest thing I ever did was…

3. I think the biggest risk for me to follow Jesus would be…

What's the biggest risk you're willing to take for Jesus this week?

4. The thing that would inconvenience me the most would be if someone were to…

5. I think the biggest inconvenience for me to follow Jesus would be…

What's one way you're willing to be inconvenienced by following Jesus this week?

THIS WEEK

The TalkSheet looks at some interesting sayings that were used in the midst of two conversations Jesus had about the cost of following him. One saying deals with taking a risk and the other with being inconvenienced. Both are realities for those who choose to follow Jesus.

OPENER

Start by having your group members come up with some slogans or memorable sayings and their meanings. Some examples are (1) "I can't walk and chew gum at the same time" (I can't do two things at once) or (2) "He has two left feet" (he isn't very coordinated). You may want to divide them into teams of two or three and make this a friendly competition with a prize for the most. Once you have your group thinking along these lines, have them look at the first question on their TalkSheets.

THE DISCUSSION, BY NUMBERS

1. Have your group read Matthew 8:18-22 either individually or in teams.
   - Verse 20 (about foxes and birds) conveys a sense of safety. Jesus is making the point that if you follow him, it can be dangerous…living without a safety net…risky.
   - Verse 21 is a Middle Eastern saying. The men in that culture would talk of "burying their fathers" to say they had family responsibilities. Men were expected to work in the family business until their father died. Then sons would receive their inheritance and be released to do as they wished. Some scholars believe this disciple was asking to stay with his family until the customary year of mourning was finished. Others believe his father wasn't dead and the disciple was saying, "It's not convenient for me to follow you now, Jesus. Maybe after I bury my father."
   - In verse 22 ("let the dead bury the dead") Jesus was basically saying, "There's never going to be a convenient time. If you keep waiting for your circumstances to change, then you'll never follow me."
2. You may want to segue with a statement like: Jesus just said some pretty risky things about following him. Ask your group to share the riskiest things they've ever done. Be careful not to glamorize any risky behaviors.
3. What risks would your students encounter if they chose to follow Jesus in their schools, families, or neighborhoods? Ask if their friends might see them differently or if their reputation might be damaged. Challenge them to think about a risk they might take this week if they chose to follow Jesus, such as sharing their faith with a friend or serving at a homeless shelter.
4. Move the discussion to the part about being inconvenienced. Encourage them to think about their relationships at home or school that might be especially inconvenient.
5. Now shift the discussion to the disciple who felt it was an inconvenient time to follow Jesus. Ask your students to think about how following Jesus might be an inconvenience in their lives today. Encourage them to think of some creative ways they could be inconvenienced while following Jesus this week, such as helping someone with her homework or visiting a sick friend.

THE CLOSE

Following Jesus will always involve risk, and it will never be convenient. The world runs counter to where Jesus is going. That's why Jesus talked about taking the narrow road that leads to life—and only a few finding it (Matthew 7:13-14). But Jesus didn't force either man to follow him. He offered and then let them choose. The same is true today: The choice is ours.

MORE

- **Show a film clip of someone in a risky situation. There's a great scene in *Jaws* where shark expert Matt Hooper (played by Richard Dreyfuss) decides the only way to kill the shark may be to get into the shark cage and inject poison into the Great White's mouth. A risky move, but he survives. (Know when to stop and start the DVD due to possibly inappropriate content.)**
- **Interview someone who has a risky job, such as a fireman or high-rise window washer. Ask them why they do what they do and how they cope with the risks involved.**
- **"Inconvenience" your students by taking them to do a service project instead of the social gathering they were expecting.**

1. The most important step in creating the world's greatest banana split is…

PEEL OFF AND CHUNK IT

2. Read Proverbs 25:4. What does the word dross mean?

3. What do removing dross and the most important step of creating a banana split have in common?

4. Read Hebrews 12:1. What are we supposed to "throw off"?

5. Why do you think throwing off such things is important (according to God)?

6. What do you think removing dross, the most important step in creating the world's greatest banana split, and throwing off what God tells us to throw off have in common?

7. The first thing I need to peel off and chunk from my life so I can be a candidate for God's blessing is…

THIS WEEK

This TalkSheet will look at two passages that call for self-examination and intentional action so God can use us. An object lesson using banana splits will drive home the point in a memorable way. (You'll need ice cream, bananas, and toppings, as well as bowls, spoons, napkins, and clean-up supplies.)

OPENER

Ask your group to create the world's greatest banana split. (At this point don't tell them they'll be creating and eating real banana splits during the group time. You want them to simply think about banana splits.) On the backside of their TalkSheets, have students describe the elements needed to create the world's greatest banana split. They should be as specific as possible about all the ingredients, including the brand and flavor of ice cream, the number of scoops, and any toppings. Have all the students share their list of elements with the group.

THE DISCUSSION, BY NUMBERS

1. The hope is that your group will overlook the most important step—peeling the bananas. If someone does get it right, affirm that without that banana-peeling step, no banana split would be very good. Until you peel the banana, it's in no position to become the world's greatest banana split. (Let your group make their banana splits at this time and then resume with the lesson as they eat them. Or complete the lesson and then do the banana-split thing at the end.)

2. Have one student read Proverbs 25:4 out loud. (Be sure the version uses the word *dross*, such as the TNIV.) Ask students to write a definition of *dross* and share it with the group. (*Dross* is the impurity found in precious metals that must be burned away so only the purity of the metal is left.) Dross represents the sin that needs to be removed before God has a pure life to work with for his own purposes.

3. Have your group members consider what removing the dross and peeling the banana have in common. Hopefully they'll make the connection that their lives are like precious metals or bananas. When we remove the parts that aren't supposed to be there, we allow God to make something great out of our lives.

4. Now have one of your students read Hebrews 12:1 out loud. Again, it's important that the version contains the words *throw off* (TNIV). Let your group answer question four: "Throw off everything that hinders and the sin that so easily entangles."

5. Ask some students to share their thoughts. Unless we "throw off" the things mentioned in this verse, we'll constantly trip and fall. God desires for us to make wise decisions so we may experience a life of victory and God's blessing.

6. Hopefully by now they see the common theme behind "removing dross," "peeling bananas," and "throwing off sin" in their lives: It's about taking responsibility for making wise and godly choices and for dealing with the sin in our lives.

7. Instead of sharing their answers with the group, they may want to share their response with just one person for accountability's sake.

THE CLOSE

If your group hasn't built their banana splits yet, let the party begin! Remember to emphasize the most important step: Peeling the bananas. If they've already enjoyed their banana splits, have them symbolically throw away their banana peels as a tangible expression of peeling off and chunking the dross, sin, and peelings that need to be discarded so God will be able to fully bless their lives.

MORE

• **Have judges determine the best banana split and award ice cream gift cards to the winners.**

• **There's a great scene in the movie *K-PAX* in which Prot (played by Kevin Spacey) eats an entire banana—peel and all. It could be a good visual reminder that only an alien or an animal would eat a banana that way.**

• **If you're looking for a way to get your adults or senior adults involved in the lives of your students, ask them to provide homemade ice cream for your gathering. Let the banana split party be an excuse for your students to enjoy some face time with adults in a fun atmosphere of eating ice cream together.**

1. If I received news that a vast army was gathering to fight against me, the first thing I'd do is…

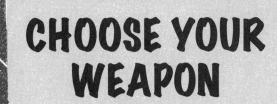

CHOOSE YOUR WEAPON

2. If I were facing an army and could choose only one weapon to fight with, it would be…

3. In 2 Chronicles 20:1, who was attacking whom?

4. In verse 3, what was the first course of action that King Jehoshaphat led all of Judah to do? Why do you think he did such a thing?

5. In verses 12 and 13, King Jehoshaphat says some things and then leads the people of Judah to do something before God. What was his confession before God? Why do you think he led the people to take that posture?

6. God used Jahaziel to speak to Jehoshaphat and his people in verses 14-17. In your own words, paraphrase what God told Jahaziel to say.

7. How did Jehoshaphat approach the battlefield in verses 21-22? When might God want you to do the same thing in your own life's battles?

THIS WEEK

Sometimes the people and situations we face in life seem to be a mounting army. In 2 Chronicles 20 we see that when armies were mounting an attack against the people of Judah, King Jehoshaphat called for a national fast and cried out to God as he led them into victory.

OPENER

Start by talking about how video games have come a long way over the last 20 years. The technology continues to become more advanced, making the world of video games more realistic and the various weapons and skills much more interesting. You might want to talk about the simplicity of some of the early video games, such as *Space Invaders* (one gun), *Missile Command* (one gun), and *Asteroids* (one gun and a force field). After a few examples from yesteryear, let your group name some of their favorites. Now ask them to write on the backside of their TalkSheets the top three weapons they've used in a video game—anything cool that they wish they could do or use

THE DISCUSSION, BY NUMBERS

1. You'll want to refer back to this question when you get to question four. Basically, you're setting up a comparison between how your students would respond and how King Jehoshaphat responded in a similar situation in 2 Chronicles 20:3. But don't refer to this verse yet.

2. You had them start their list of weapons in the Opener. Now they must narrow it down to only one weapon.

3. Read 2 Chronicles 20:1-30 before continuing the discussion. Challenge your group to think of it as the plot for a new video game. As you read, ask them to think about what it might look like on a screen, and then ask them to come up with a name for the new video game.

4. Explain what a "fast" is and why it was important as a sign of total dependence and trust in God. Fasting was a way for people to demonstrate how desperate they were for God to speak to them or do something on their behalf. Have them look back at what they wrote for question one and notice how different their approaches were.

5. Jehoshaphat declared that he saw the difficult situation his people were in. He confessed he didn't know what to do and so the best option was to look to God for help. Such a posture was one of great expectations. Such confessions were clearly seen as being in total dependence on God.

6. In a sense God told Jahaziel to say, "Hey, chill out! I've got your back." Have someone read verses 14 through 17 aloud and then give them a few minutes to jot down their answers to the question.

7. The weapon Jehoshaphat used was rather unconventional: A choir. The troops chose to fight with worship since God was going before them into battle. Ask someone to read verses 21-22. Then take a few minutes to hear some responses from your group as you wrap up your discussion.

THE CLOSE

Regardless of the situation, it's always an appropriate response to worship. However, it's especially appropriate when things are out of our hands. In fact, it's often when we try to do things in our own strength and power that we wind up feeling overconfident, which usually leads to humiliation and loss. Sometimes the best things we can do are fast, call on God, listen to his voice, and respond with worship from our lips and our lives.

MORE

• **Challenge your group to enter into some type of non-food fast for the coming week. You can abstain from anything, such as television, cell phones, music, and video games. Get creative, but remember to do it with purpose.**

• **Talk through various ways your group might intentionally worship God as they go about their days in the coming week. Read the Psalms out loud as a confession back to God, write a letter of thanksgiving to God, start and end the day with a time of singing praise to God, listen to praise music and dance before God, or serve someone in the name of Jesus.**

• **Set up a video game tournament as a way to fellowship and reach out to new students. In the middle of the tournament, call a time-out and work through the TalkSheet before finishing the tournament.**

1. Check out Luke 4:16. What was one of Jesus' habits or customs?

HABITS

2. Why do you think this habit was a part of Jesus' life that he never broke?

3. Take a look at one of Paul's habits in Acts 17:2 and write it here.

4. Turn over to Hebrews 10:24-25 and jot down the habit that God wants you to make a part of your life.

5. According to Luke 4:16, Acts 17:2, and Hebrews 10:24-25, what kinds of things went on at these meetings? Finish your list by adding the habits found in Acts 2:42.

6. How might these habits affect your life if you made them your custom like Jesus, Paul, and followers of Jesus from the early days of the New Testament?

THIS WEEK

Your students will not only consider the subject of habits, but also take a look at one of the habits of Jesus and his followers: Meeting together for worship. Things that were habitual for Jesus are always worth considering making a habit in our own lives.

OPENER

You may want to get your group thinking about habits by simply making the statement that **Habits are a part of human nature**. Let them know you're going to talk about four kinds of habits, then give an example of each type: bad—chewing fingernails; good—saying "please" and "thank you"; neutral—combing your hair before brushing your teeth; and gross—picking your nose. Give your group a few minutes to make their own lists of good, bad, neutral, and gross habits on the backside of their TalkSheets. Feel free to take some time with this because you want them to really think about habits before you get to the questions concerning a habit of Jesus, Paul, and the followers of Jesus.

THE DISCUSSION, BY NUMBERS

1. Share that even Jesus had habits. Have the group read Luke 4:16. That word for *custom* can also be translated as "habit." It's a Greek noun that gives us our English word *ethos*. In the four places where it refers to Jesus' life in the Gospels, it always revolves around the act of worship or teaching the people about God.

2. It was the habit or custom of the Jews to *always* keep the Sabbath day by worshiping at the local synagogue. This is how Jesus was raised and how Jesus' ancestors were raised since the time of Moses. Going to corporate worship was their custom; it was a part of their ethos that was embedded into their DNA. Jesus continued to model the importance of keeping the Sabbath day holy by remembering God and worshiping him in a public setting with fellow God-lovers.

3. Now have your group look at one of Paul's habits as they turn over to Acts 17:2. Again we see this same phrase: "As was his custom." It's the same word that was used in Luke 4:16.

4. Going to church to worship God with other believers is a big deal to God. Hebrews 10:24-25 shows that some people had gotten out of the "habit" of meeting together to remember the Sabbath day and worship

God. But in God's eyes, it's vitally important for those who claim to love God not to give up worshiping God as a corporate body.

5. Have your group members go back to those three Bible verses—Luke 4:16, Acts 17:2, and Hebrews 10:24-25—and write what was taking place at church: Reading the Scriptures, teaching and discussing the Scriptures, and encouraging one another. Then have them look over Acts 2:42 for additional elements: Devoting themselves to the apostles' teaching, fellowship, breaking bread (the Lord's Supper as well as fellowship meals), and praying together.

6. Wrap up the discussion by asking how it might affect their lives if they were to become habitual in some of the same practices found in these verses. There are no wrong answers. Wrap up your time with a challenge to implement some of these habits into their own lives over the next few weeks.

THE CLOSE

It's clear that God desires for his followers to worship with others. The location can vary, but it's intended to be done corporately and consistently wherever the church is meeting. Ask your group to make a commitment to return next week and continue meeting together, as was the habit of Jesus, Paul, and the early followers.

MORE

• **Between meeting times, encourage your group to make it a habit to pray for one another as they did in Acts 2:42. They may want to support one another throughout the week with words of affirmation in the halls at school, text messages to let them know they're praying for one another, or even notes of encouragement.**

• **Ask your group to commit to memorize Hebrews 10:25. Challenge them to stop and pray for each other or text one another with a simple "10:25" at 10:25 a.m. and 10:25 p.m. as a way to encourage and hold one another accountable.**

• **Get wristbands or bracelets similar to the LIVESTRONG bracelets and write "10:25" on them as part of a new campaign for your group. These could be not only a great way to build unity, but also a great conversation piece among friends and acquaintances who don't know Jesus.**

1. What do you think Jesus was talking about when he said "living water" and why do you think his statements connected with the woman?

2. Take a close look at verses 16-18. If the woman had been throwing coins into that well and making wishes every time she came to draw water, based on her conversation with Jesus, what do you think she would have wished for?

3. Up to verse 18 in the story, would you describe the woman as being thirsty or satisfied in her heart and soul?

4. If you had to use one of those two words to describe yourself, what's the true state of your heart and soul today: Thirsty or satisfied?

5. If you were sitting next to Jesus and you had one wish, what would you wish for?

6. Do you think your wish and what Jesus wants you to wish for would be the same thing? If so, why? If not, why not—and what would Jesus want you to wish for instead?

THIS WEEK

Today's TalkSheet will focus on a story that takes place by a well. The discussion is meant to draw your group into seeing this well as a "wishing well" to help them talk through things they "wish for" versus committing their desires to prayer.

OPENER

Begin this discussion with an object lesson by using a roll of pennies and either a bucket of water or a small wading pool. You might even hold your group discussion next to a fountain or other body of water. The idea is that each time a student shares an answer, she drops a penny into the water. You may want to give each person only one penny and have them hold onto it until the end of the discussion. If you decide to have them toss multiple pennies throughout the discussion, it may work better to keep the pennies in a bowl near the water and have the students take a penny and toss it into the water when it's their turn to share. To start off, ask, **If you could throw a coin into a wishing well and have your wish come true, what would you wish for?**

THE DISCUSSION, BY NUMBERS

1. Now that they're thinking about this whole concept of "making wishes," segue by letting them know they'll be looking at Jesus' conversation with a woman next to a well. Have them turn to John 4 and read the start of this story in verses 4-15. "Living water" describes water from a moving source. Jesus knew that if the woman were able to find a source for living water, she wouldn't have to work so hard to provide water for her household. He addressed her physical needs before he touched her emotional needs.

2. Jesus goes straight to the woman's wish for security, identity, and fulfillment through a relationship with a man. The woman hadn't said anything about her current relationship. Jesus knew what was going on inside her heart, soul, and life. He knows the longing of our hearts, too.

3. This woman had a thirsty heart and soul, but she tried to quench her thirst by going to the false wells of relationships and intimacy.

4. Give your group a moment to think and encourage them to be gut-level honest. Ask them to write their answer and a few words to explain why.

5. Your group could be very vulnerable when answering questions five and six. Challenge them to take it seriously.

6. Ask your students to put themselves in Jesus' shoes. What would his wish for them be? Would it be the same thing they wished for? Encourage them to think deeply about their answer.

THE CLOSE

Take a moment to summarize what happened after the woman went back to her family (vv. 19-42). Her thirsty soul became so quenched by the life of Jesus that her whole family came out to meet him, and they became believers as well. Encourage your students to begin thinking of their wishes as desires to pray about. Challenge them to ask God to make their desires match up with God's desires for their lives. As they leave, give them each a penny to remind them to move from wishing to praying. Ask them to carry the pennies as a reminder to pray constantly about the things God would have them desire. Holding the pennies could also help them stay intentional during their conversations with God.

MORE

• **Commit to a service project or act of kindness that "makes someone's wish come true." Ask local hospital personnel or a city council member about specific needs they're aware of that your group could act upon as an expression of kindness and blessing in making someone's wish come true.**

• **Sponsor a child through Compassion International and "make his wish come true" as a group effort. Choose to financially support the child together as a way of regularly focusing on someone who is less fortunate.**

• **One thing people always say before someone blows out their birthday candles is, "Make a wish!" Throw a birthday party with a cake and candles for elderly people in a retirement or nursing home. Sing songs with them and visit them as an expression of love.**

• **Study what Jesus said in John 7:37-38 about anyone who is thirsty coming to Jesus to drink. You might also want to look at the theme of water and thirst in Psalm 42 and Psalm 23.**

1. **Make a list of all the superheroes you can think of, as well as their superpowers.**

SUPERHERO-SUPERPOWER

2. **Of all the superheroes listed, rank your top three superpowers in the order you wish you had them and give a reason for why you wish you had each one.**

    a.

    b.

    c.

3. **In our world what things cause someone to be known as a powerful person?**

4. **What does the Bible say about power?**

    • Ephesians 3:14-21

    • Colossians 1:29

    • Hebrews 1:1-3

    • James 5:16

5. **What do you think God might want you to do to become a person of power based on these passages?**

THIS WEEK

Middle schoolers often feel powerless. They can't drive yet. They're too young to date. They have late curfews. And they're experiencing the awkward stages of puberty. This TalkSheet will lead your group through a discussion of what it means to live a life of power.

OPENER

Begin your time by talking about how cool it would be to have the superpowers of superheroes. You may even want to talk about the recent surge of movies that have focused on such superheroes as Spider-Man, Iron Man, the Hulk, and Batman. If you have access to a computer that your group can gather around, it may be helpful to pull up Web sites about superheroes. (Two excellent ones are *http://shdictionary.tripod.com* and *www.comicvine.com*.) As you mention these first few examples, project their images onto the screen for added visual effect. However, keep in mind that your group will soon be making a list of their favorite superheroes and their powers, so be careful not to give away too many. As your group walks through the discussion, you can display the images of their favorite superheroes to help engage your group in the discussion.

THE DISCUSSION, BY NUMBERS

1. Now that your group is thinking about superheroes and their superpowers, give them a few moments to write down as many as they can. Then compile a master list on a whiteboard or large sheet of paper. Feel free to find more superheroes from the Web sites mentioned above, if necessary.

2. After your group has shared their lists from question one, have them answer question two using the master list you've just created.

3. This question turns the conversation toward real people who are considered powerful. Have them share their answers with the group and make a second master list. Some possible answers include money, family, intelligence, strength, or physical stature.

4. The following verses all specifically talk about "power" in the TNIV.
   - Ephesians 3:14-21 refers to the power that followers of Jesus receive from the Holy Spirit living inside of them, including the power to truly understand the love God has for his children.
   - Colossians 1:29 speaks of the energy of Christ powerfully working in the life of Paul as he continues to work for the gospel in his community.
   - Hebrews 1:1-3 speaks of the power that's found in the Word of God.
   - James 5:16 speaks of the power of prayers from righteous people.

5. Other places in the Bible, such as 2 Timothy 1:7, also speak of power and how it's meant to be lived out in the lives of believers. Help your group members think about how such power could become a reality in their own lives. You want your students to see that God desires for them to incorporate the powerful things of God into their lives (becoming a person of prayer, reading and internalizing the words of the Bible, growing in the knowledge of God, and living a life that's yielded to the Holy Spirit).

THE CLOSE

Ask if Jesus was a person of power. Then point out that Jesus didn't let his power go to his head. In fact Philippians 2:1-11 offers a great snapshot of how Jesus lived a life of humility and service as he loved others and fulfilled his God-given purpose on earth. Jesus' life offers the greatest illustration of power being lived out in a way that honors God and serves mankind. Challenge your students to do likewise this week.

MORE

• **Ask your group to come dressed as their favorite superhero and award prizes for the most creative costumes.**

• **Let your students come up with a group hand signal for "power." Encourage them to flash the "power" sign whenever they see each other during the week as a reminder to live a life of power in Christ.**

• **Host a superhero-movie-watching party as an outreach event so your students can invite their friends who don't attend church. Then lead this TalkSheet discussion at some point during the evening. Some great movies to consider are *Spider-Man, Fantastic Four, X-Men, The Hulk, Ghost Rider, Batman, Teenage Mutant Ninja Turtles, The Incredibles,* and *Superman*. As always, some movies may not be appropriate for all audiences. Use discretion and make sure the parents are okay with whatever movies you plan to show to the group.**

1. Take 10 minutes and write down as much of the Bible as you can from memory.

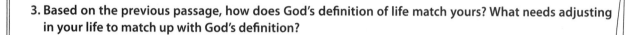

MEMORY

2. Read Deuteronomy 32:45-47. On a scale of 1 to 10, with 10 being the best score, how much "life" is inside of you? Explain your answer.

3. Based on the previous passage, how does God's definition of life match yours? What needs adjusting in your life to match up with God's definition?

4. Read Psalm 119:11. What does this mean and why do you think it has such a powerful effect on the way you live your life?

5. Read Psalm 119:105. What do you think this verse is saying and how do you think it might change your life if you knew more of God's Word (the Bible)?

6. How do you think your life would be different if you memorized one Bible verse a week?

THIS WEEK

The goal of this TalkSheet is to show your students the value of knowing the Bible. This session should allow your group to see just how much they can remember, along with how much (or how little) of the Bible they have committed to memory.

OPENER

This Opener should take more time than usual. Divide your group into teams with at least two people on a team. Then set the stage by letting your students know you're going to test their memories. Start off by asking them to write down as many phone numbers as they can. Then ask them to write other bits of information, such as their friends' locker combinations, the names and jersey numbers of professional athletes, or all of the movies starring certain actors (such as Tom Hanks). Next, play a portion of a popular song and have the teams either write out the lyrics or sing the very next line. These games will help your students recognize that they have the ability to remember all kinds of information.

Now ask your students this question: "On a scale of 1 to 10, with 10 being the most important, how important is the Bible to you?" Whatever your students say, be affirming. You'll soon see if what they say and what they do match up.

Ask your teams to pretend they've just moved to a foreign country where it's illegal to be a Christian. All of the churches are "underground," and if the authorities catch them worshiping or carrying a Bible, they'll be thrown in jail—perhaps worse. Your group is committed to following Jesus but must do so covertly. The authorities have been conducting raids in the area, so your church decided that all Bibles should be buried in a secret place. Your group must now rely upon their memories if they want to know what the Bible says. Have them answer the first question on their TalkSheets now.

THE DISCUSSION, BY NUMBERS

1. Suggest that they start with any Bible verses they've memorized and then move on to any stories and teachings. After 10 minutes is up, have the teams share what they could remember. This will likely show just how much they don't have committed to memory.
2. Have your students read Deuteronomy 32:45-47 and give themselves a score from 1 to 10, with 10 being best. Moses says God's words are to be the very life of the people of God. How much "life" do your students have? Ask a few volunteers to explain the reasoning behind their scores.
3. After your students have compared God's definition of life with theirs, have them talk through any adjustments they'd need to make so their definitions line up with God's.
4. Have them read Psalm 119:11 and determine what it means. How would a person do this? Are there tricks to memorizing Scripture? How can knowing what God says affect a person's choice to sin?
5. Now ask them to consider Psalm 119:105. Have them offer some examples as to how they'd live differently.
6. How do they think their lives would be different in one month, in six months, in one year, in six years… and so on?

THE CLOSE

Encourage your group to take the "Bible Memory Verse Challenge." For the next six weeks, select a weekly verse for your group to memorize, such as Deuteronomy 6:5, Psalm 51:10, Jeremiah 29:11, Matthew 6:33, Mark 10:45, John 10:10, Acts 4:12, Romans 10:9-10, Philippians 2:5, 1 Timothy 4:12, Hebrews 11:6, or 1 John 1:9.

MORE

• **Either in your meeting room or a nearby space, create an "underground church" atmosphere by darkening the room, lighting some candles, and playing Gregorian chant music. Give each team a candle to huddle around while they answer their questions on the TalkSheet.**
• **Give your group a different hypothetical to consider: Being stranded on a deserted island without a Bible. They must colonize the island because they'll never leave it. And it's up to them to remember as much as they can from the Bible and pass on their knowledge to their children (and their children's children) so future generations can have a relationship with Jesus.**
• **Invite the parents to participate in this session. It could be a very revealing time for them to see just how much their children do or don't know when it comes to Scripture. It may also motivate and challenge them to make learning Scripture a priority for their children, as well as for themselves.**

1. Who are the top five most influential people in your life?

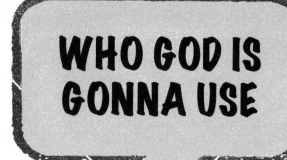

WHO GOD IS GONNA USE

2. Not including anybody named in the Bible, who's influenced more people to become followers of Jesus than anyone else since Jesus' resurrection? Why?

3. What was significant about a man named Mordecai Ham?

4. Listen to the song "Who God Is Gonna Use" by Rich Mullins and then look up the names listed in the song lyrics to find out how God used them.

- Balaam's Donkey (Numbers 22:21-34)

- A princess (Exodus 2:1-10)

- Esther and Mordecai (Esther 3–8…Let your leader summarize this one.)

- Miriam (Exodus 15:19-21)

- Jubal (Genesis 4:21)

- Samson (Judges 16:18-30)

- Pontius Pilate (John 18:32–19:16)

5. What's the name of one person whom you think God might want you to influence this week? How?

THIS WEEK
For this TalkSheet discussion, you'll need a CD player and the Rich Mullins song "Who God Is Gonna Use" so you can play it for your group. You'll also want to provide a copy of the lyrics so your students can follow along *(www.kidbrothers.net/wabairi1.html#wgigu).*

OPENER
Start by talking about how tattoos have become more popular in mainstream culture and then show some pictures of famous people with tattoos. On the backside of their TalkSheets, have each person sketch the tattoo they'd get if they had to get one. It must be at least two inches by two inches big. Ask volunteers to share what they'd get and where they'd have it tattooed on their body. After you have them thinking about tattoos, jump into question one. (Note: This isn't a TalkSheet about tattoos. It's simply meant to engage your students and lead them into a discussion of how God can use your students to influence others.)

THE DISCUSSION, BY NUMBERS
1. Have them list the top five most influential people in their lives and why. You may want to take the lead by sharing your top five.
2. Emphasize that this person is *not* in the Bible. Hopefully someone will say Billy Graham. (So if you're offering examples, don't include him.) Billy has shared the gospel with more than 210 million people in 185 countries. However, before he influenced even one person for Jesus, someone influenced Billy's life during a revival in 1934: Mordecai Ham.
3. Let them guess who Mordecai Ham is and perhaps give a prize for the most creative. Then help them make the connection between how God used Mordecai to influence Billy who then influenced millions of people around the world. Say something like—**You never know who God will use to influence the lives of others for his purposes.**
4. Before you play "Who God Is Gonna Use," pass out copies of the lyrics and encourage your students to think about the people mentioned in the song. After the song ends, divide your students into smaller groups and assign one of the Bible passages to each one. Have them read the Scripture and write how that person's (animal's) life was used to influence others.
   - Balaam's Donkey: He saw the angel of the Lord and kept Balaam from certain death.

- Princess: Pharaoh's daughter unknowingly saved the life of baby Moses who would grow up and lead the people of Israel out of Egypt.
- Esther and Mordecai: God allowed a beautiful Jewish woman to become the wife of the king who wasn't Jewish. Meanwhile, a wicked official in the king's court, named Haman, creates a decree to have all Jewish people killed. Mordecai, Esther's uncle, asks Esther to plead with the king for mercy. God uses Esther to influence the king not only to spare the lives of the Jews, but also to honor Mordecai and kill Haman.
- Miriam: Moses' sister led the women in dancing and singing praises to God for bringing them through the Red Sea safely.
- Jubal: The father of all who played stringed instruments and pipes.
- Samson: With God's strength, he pushed down the pillars of the temple, killing the Philistine rulers and all the people inside.
- Pontius Pilate: His decision to have Jesus crucified influenced the soldiers to carry out the orders that would give life and hope to the world through the death of Jesus.

5. Get your group thinking about the fact that God might want to use their lives to influence other people. Have your students write the first initial of the person they believe God wants them to influence. Then have them consider *how* God may want to use them in the coming week.

THE CLOSE
Remind them that God can use anybody and everybody—even a donkey—to influence others and do the will of God. Challenge them to make themselves available to be used by God. Close your time by praying for your group.

MORE
- **Have your students write letters of appreciation to the five most influential people in their lives and mail them.**
- **Challenge your group to take one of the stories listed in question four and read it as part of their daily devotion and prayer time.**
- **Challenge your group to send each other secret code text messages throughout the week: A capital N to remind them to pray and be available for God to use them as iNfluencers in their world.**

1. Describe the difference between a gaze and a glance.

   • A *gaze* is…

   • A *glance* is…

BOUNCE YOUR EYES

2. Check out 2 Samuel 11:1-5. What did King David see? Do you think he gazed or glanced? Why?

3. Give an example of how a poor choice can lead from a seemingly harmless action into a situation with heavy consequences.

4. What could David have done to prevent this course of action?

5. How could Bathsheba have made sure this situation never occurred?

6. Read Job 31:1. If David had memorized this verse, what influence might it have had on him?

7. Where will you most likely need to "bounce your eyes" this week?

THIS WEEK

Your group will discuss two different approaches to viewing temptations—an intentional gaze or an inadvertent glance—and strategies to help them choose wisely. Ultimately, one of the best strategies is to "bounce the eyes" away from the temptation and onto something else.

OPENER

Start by having your group pair off for an old-fashioned staring contest. The rules are simple: Each person must face one other person. On the count of three, the pairs will begin staring into each other's eyes until one of them blinks or turns away. Feel free to make it an elimination tournament with the "blinkers" from each round being eliminated until only one contestant remains. After a champion is named, have your group take a look at the TalkSheet.

THE DISCUSSION, BY NUMBERS

1. A *gaze* is intently staring at an object in your sightline. A *glance* is a quick or inadvertent look at something in your sightline. Have your students share their definitions with the rest of the group.

2. Have someone read 2 Samuel 11:1-5 aloud, then give your students a few moments to answer question two. David saw a naked woman taking a bath, and it was definitely a gaze. David could tell this woman was *very* beautiful, and he wanted to find out more about her. If it were only a glance, he wouldn't have gone to such lengths. Something to note: David was merely out for a stroll and saw a sight that caused him to gaze. However, according to verse 1, King David was *supposed* to be at war. When we have idle time on our hands, it's easy to make sinful choices.

3. Challenge your students to think deeply about this question. One example is how viewing inappropriate images on a computer may go from lust to pornographic addiction. Another might be going to a party where there could be drugs or drinking and "trying it just once," which could lead to more experimentation and ultimately addiction.

4. Have your students answer questions four and five before sharing with the group. David certainly could have chosen *not* to gaze at Bathsheba. Perhaps if David had known that a friend would be asking him if he'd been sexually pure, he would have glanced

instead of gazed. David also could have asked his servants to tell Bathsheba to bathe somewhere else.

5. Bathsheba could have had more accountability in her life by asking her friends to help her stay faithful to her husband. She also could have bathed inside the house.

6. Job 31:1 says, "I made a covenant with my eyes not to look lustfully at a girl." When we're faced with temptation, God reminds us of the Scriptures we've memorized. (Cf. Psalm 119:11—"I have hidden your word in my heart that I might not sin against you.") Had David memorized this verse in Job, he might have remembered his promise not to do such a thing and chosen to "bounce his eyes." Think of someone watching a tennis match—their eyes bounce from one side of the net to the other. It's the same idea. Whenever temptation comes into our sightlines, we can choose to "bounce our eyes" onto something else.

7. Give your group a few moments to think about places where sin and temptation are likely to fall into their sightlines this week—on their computers, on television, a crush at school, when they're out shopping. Ask them to share their answers with one another to finish up the discussion.

THE CLOSE

Close the session by encouraging your group to pair up with someone who will simply ask them how they're doing with the issue they named in question seven. With accountability we're more likely to bounce our eyes and avoid destructive choices.

MORE

• **Give each student a bouncy ball as a reminder to bounce their eyes when temptation enters their sightlines.**

• **Ask an adult to share her story of how the progression of sin, perhaps involving drugs or alcohol or even sexual choices, caused devastating results in her life. Reading a story in the Bible and then hearing about a modern-day example of how these same progressions unfold in ways that teenagers can relate to can make a big impact on your students.**

• **Incorporate some video games that involve shooting an object in the player's sightline. Old-school games such as *Duck Hunt* come to mind, but ask your students for some current, and appropriate, examples.**

1. If you knew you had only one more meal on Earth, what would be on the menu?

TASTY!

2. List as many foods as you can think of that taste good to you.

3. List as many foods as you can think of that taste bad to you.

4. What words describe foods that taste good?

5. What words describe foods that taste bad?

6. If they had to choose at least one word from your lists in questions four and five, which word would the following people choose to describe the way your life "tastes"? Why?
   • You:

   • Your friends:

   • Your family:

   • Your teachers:

7. Write down Psalm 34:8. How do you think God wants you to do the first part of that verse?

8. What does it take for a person to live a life that "tastes good" to God?

9. What does it take for a person to live a life that "tastes bad" to God?

10. How might tasting the goodness of God change the way your life tastes?

THIS WEEK

This TalkSheet will help your group process what it means to "Taste and see that the Lord is good." Middle schoolers are often like garbage disposals: They'll typically eat anything you put in front of them. Use food to engage them with a powerful Psalm that could change the flavor of their lives.

OPENER

Have your group answer the first question on their Talk-Sheets. Make it a scenario if you like. Tell them you've been given insider information from God, and today is the last day of Earth as we know it. Thus, they have one meal left to enjoy, and no food is off-limits. After they share their menus, tell them that individuals on death row really do get a "last meal."

THE DISCUSSION, BY NUMBERS

1. After the group shares their answers, read some last-meal requests from *www.deadmaneating.com*. (You probably don't want to mention this Web site as part of the discussion.)

2. Ask them to complete questions two and three before discussing their answers with the group. The goal is to get them thinking about foods that taste good, as well as bad.

3. See question two.

4. Now have them answer questions four and five. Offer a few examples to prime the pump: *juicy, savory, flavorful, hearty, spicy*, and so on.

5. See question four. Descriptive words for foods that taste bad include *bland, tough, dry, smoky, gross, fatty*, and so on.

6. Challenge your group to go deeper as they consider how their lives have a particular "taste" or flavor. Then have each student select one of the words listed in questions four and five to describe how the four groups of people would describe how the student's life "tastes." Feel free to add other groups that might be appropriate, but don't mention Jesus or God just yet. Whatever words they choose, make sure they give their reasons.

7. Now have them write down Psalm 34:8. We're focusing on the first phrase: "Taste and see that the Lord is good." How can a person taste the goodness of God? Hopefully they'll talk about being obedient and living the way God instructs us in the Bible.

8. Have them answer questions eight and nine together. You want them to internalize Psalm 34:8. Their answers may include things like issues of obedience, honesty, being humble and kind, and so on.

9. See question eight.

10. This question will probably stretch your group. Explore their answers but be cautious about answering it for them. If they can't come up with something, challenge them to chew on it during the week or ask their parents or friends what they think. Once a person has tasted the goodness of God, he craves more of who God is and what God is about. Thus, you are what you eat!

THE CLOSE

Close by giving each person a tasty food as a reminder of the goodness and sweetness of God. It might be a delicious chocolate or a sweet candy. Let them savor it as you pray for them.

MORE

• Split your group into two teams and see how quickly two contestants can consume various foods that taste good and taste bad. Have the dishes covered so contestants don't know whether it'll be a good- or bad-tasting food until it's placed before them.

• Start off with a game called "Eat That Food" that's based on the game show *Name That Tune*. However, players will see a food item (such as a plate of cookies) and challenge each other regarding the amount of time it will take to consume it. One contestant may say: "I can eat that food in 20 seconds." The challenger may then either lower the amount of time (if she thinks she can eat the food in less time) or say, "Eat that food!" if she thinks it will take her opponent longer than 20 seconds to finish eating.

1. In the children's game Follow the Leader, what makes someone a "good leader" versus a "bad leader"?

FOLLOW THE LEADER

2. Write down 1 Corinthians 11:1. Why do you think Paul made this statement?

3. What do you think the life of a person your age would look like in order for her to make a statement like Paul's?

4. Describe what the life of a person your age would look like if she were considered a "bad example" to follow if people wanted to be like Jesus.

5. How do you think people can get to a place in their lives where they're considered good leaders or examples of people who live for Jesus?

6. Read Matthew 4:18-20. Jesus called Peter and Andrew to follow him. If Jesus walked into the room right now and said to you, "Come, follow me," what would be different about your situation? What would be the same?

   • Different:

   • Same:

7. What area of your life is the most like Jesus so others could follow it as an example?

8. What area of your life needs some work to be more like Jesus before others could follow you as an example?

THIS WEEK

This main point of the discussion is what it means to be a person who's worthy of being followed. Paul tells the Christians in Corinth to follow his example as he follows Christ. "Follow the Leader" will get your group thinking about what makes a good leader and a not-so-good leader.

OPENER

Bring out some old-school games for them to play, such as Operation, Hungry-Hungry Hippos, Don't Break the Ice, and Pick-Up Sticks. After some time, ask them to think about the games they played in preschool and elementary school and name their favorites, as well as the ones they didn't enjoy playing. Examples might include card games like Memory and Go Fish, video games, and simple games such as Hide-and-Seek and Leap Frog. Share a few of your favorites and then turn their attention to the TalkSheet.

The Discussion, By Numbers

1. Share how to play Follow the Leader so your students have it fresh in their minds: One person is the "leader" and the others simply follow him and do whatever he does. Discuss what makes a "good leader" and a "bad leader" in this game. Being a "good leader" might mean going over and around playground equipment and at the right speed. A "bad leader" might mean walking in a straight line or going too fast or too slow.

2. In 1 Corinthians 11:1, Paul tells the Christians in Corinth that if they want their lives to bring honor and glory to Jesus, they should follow Paul's example as he follows the example of Jesus. Paul was confident in knowing what it took to be a follower of Jesus. He knew the Scriptures. He'd experienced a life-changing moment with Jesus on the Road to Damascus. He'd talked with Jesus' disciples. He'd been persecuted for his faith and remained true to his convictions. He knew how to pray and how to share Christ with others.

3. Help your students bring the concepts from question two into their lives today. Ask them to answer questions three and four together. Make sure they know they don't have to be perfect to be a good example, but they do have to be faithful to Jesus—in public and in private. Let your group discuss these questions in smaller groups and then share their answers with the whole group.

4. See question three.

5. Some may feel inadequate to be a leader worth following. Let them answer the question but make sure you encourage them that true discipleship takes a lifetime. It's a daily commitment to be like Jesus. It happens by doing the little things in life with excellence and integrity.

6. Have your group look up Matthew 4:18-20 where Jesus calls Peter and Andrew to "Come, follow me." How might your students respond if Jesus walked into the room and said the same thing to them? What would be different between their situation and Peter and Andrew's? (Peter and Andrew were older. They had jobs and weren't in school.) What would be the same? (Jesus extends that same call to all people regardless of their age and responsibilities. Following Jesus will always cost something.)

7. As you get to the end of the TalkSheet, ask your group to answer questions seven and eight together. You want them to think about the attribute of their life that's worth following, as well as an area in their lives that could use some work. Let them share both as you wrap up your time together in this discussion.

8. See question seven.

THE CLOSE

Encourage your group by sharing that following Jesus is an every-moment-of-every-day kind of lifestyle. One must earn the right to be followed. Challenge them to work on that one thing they mentioned in question eight, as well as strengthening the attribute from question seven in humility. Close your time by praying over your group.

MORE
• Incorporate a game of Follow the Leader into the start of the session.
• Have a leader from your community share her perspective on what it takes to be a great leader who's also committed to being a follower of Jesus.
• If you want to use a different object lesson, have someone who knows how to tie knots teach your students how to tie various types of knots step by step. Good leaders make sure others are following them and know what's being asked of them. A bad leader goes too fast and doesn't clearly demonstrate how to proceed.

THE DOMINO EFFECT

1. Which domino do you think was the most important one and why?

2. Check out John 6:1-13. Which character is a great candidate for the first domino? Why?

3. How did this person's actions affect the lives of others?

4. What qualified this person to be used by Jesus in such a way?

5. How did Jesus respond to this person and what was Jesus' part in the domino effect?

6. Why did Jesus ask, "Where shall we buy bread for these people to eat?" in verse 5? (Look at verse 6.)

7. What question is Jesus asking you about circumstances in your life, school, family, or world?

8. What's your answer to his question?

THIS WEEK

A little boy gave his lunch to Jesus, not realizing that God would use it to feed the multitudes of hungry people. God is looking for ordinary people to simply offer what they have to Jesus and start a domino effect that will impact lives in ways that only God could imagine.

OPENER

Give your group as many dominos as you can find and let them set up a design of their choosing that will be toppled before you begin the TalkSheet discussion. Consider dividing your group into teams and have each team create their own designs. The main object of this activity is to make sure the "domino effect" is clearly seen. The domino effect is when one domino is toppled, thus causing a chain reaction that topples the rest of the dominos. You could also show your group one of the many amazing domino videos on YouTube.

THE DISCUSSION, BY NUMBERS

1. This is an opinion question so just make sure they have sound reasoning for their answers. Hopefully, they'll talk about the first domino to fall. If the first one doesn't fall, then the rest would never move. Thus, that first domino is key.

2. Give your group a chance to read the story in John 6:1-13. As you set up the story, share how most scholars believe that if the women and children present had been counted, there easily could have been more than 20,000 people in attendance! Hopefully, your students will recognize the little boy in verse 9 as the lead domino. He offered Jesus all he had.

3. Because the little boy offered himself—and his lunch—Jesus took this boy's gift and fed the masses in a miraculous way. Sometimes all God desires is that we make our lives available. Jesus already knew what he was going to do, but he loves it when we choose to become a part of his plans to meet the needs of those around us.

4. The little boy was willing to be used by Jesus.

5. Jesus gave thanks for what the little boy offered and began distributing the food until all of the people were full—and there were leftovers! Jesus was the "middle domino" in this event. He waited until the first domino (the little boy) "fell forward" in faith before feeding the crowd.

6. Sometimes Jesus asks questions to see how those around him will respond. In this case, verse 6 says he was "testing" Philip. Jesus wanted to see who trusted him. Jesus wanted to see who would make themselves available to be used by God in dealing with the situation at hand. Jesus always knows the answers. However, he sometimes wants us to participate in finding the solution to the problem.

7. Encourage your students to think about their relationships at home, school, or perhaps on a team or in extracurricular activities. It might be helpful for you to offer an example from your own life, such as dealing with a family member whom God wants you to encourage or helping your neighbor with something. Let your group think about their particular situations in life and then give them time to share their answers with one another.

8. For this final question, give them an opportunity simply to write down their response to Jesus' question, as most will likely say, "Yes."

THE CLOSE

Wrap up your time by giving each person a domino to take home with them as a reminder to make themselves available to God. Then pray that they'd choose to make themselves available to Jesus just as the little boy in the story did. Pray that they'd live lives that are consistently available to Jesus and be ready to respond with a "yes life," regardless of what the question may be.

MORE

• **Take your group to McDonald's or Long John Silver's for lunch and have everybody order fish sandwiches as a way to remember the story of the five loaves and two fish.**

• **At the beginning of your time, play music by Fats Domino to add atmosphere to the concept of the domino effect.**

• **Have everyone download the Van Morrison song "Domino" into their MP3 players or as a ringtone on their cell phones, and let it serve as a theme song for the week.**

• **Challenge your group to take their domino with them everywhere they go this week as a constant reminder to be on the lookout for opportunities to institute the domino effect in whatever ways Jesus might wish to use them to impact others for good.**

1. Who are the four people on earth whom you know better than anyone else?

I KNOW YOU

2. Who are the four people on the earth who know you better than anyone else?

3. Check out Jeremiah 1:4-5. What does that say about what's known about you?

4. What's one thing you're glad God knows about you?

5. What's one thing you wish God didn't know about you?

6. Read those verses in Jeremiah 1:4-5 again. What do you think God has set you apart for?

7. If you could know one thing about your life that God knows, what would it be?

8. Since God knows everything about your life—past, present, and future—how does that truth affect the way you should respond to God with your life?

THIS WEEK

This discussion revolves around the concept of knowing and being known by others. It ultimately leads to how we're fully known by the God of the universe who created us and knew us before we ever lived.

OPENER

Grab some current issues of popular magazines—such as *US*, *People*, *Entertainment Weekly*, *Sports Illustrated*, and *Rolling Stone*—and cut out several pictures of celebrities. Put the pictures on a piece of poster board and number them. (Be sure to make yourself an answer key.) As your group gathers, have them number the backside of their TalkSheets and write the names of all the people they can identify from the celebrity montage you've created. After a few minutes, go over it together and let them name each of the celebrities. See who got the most right and give that student a prize before you dig into the TalkSheet.

THE DISCUSSION, BY NUMBERS

1. Now that you have them thinking about people they can identify, ask your students to name the four people they know better than anyone else on earth.

2. Now shift the question to the four people who know them better than anyone else. Let them share their answers with the group.

3. Have your group read Jeremiah 1:4-5. This passage speaks specifically about the prophet Jeremiah. However, the principle applies to all people. Basically, God has known us fully since before God formed us in our mothers' wombs. God also knew the outcome of our lives before we took our first breath.

4. Have your group answer questions four and five together and then share both answers before the next person goes. Take mental notes based on their answers to question five and encourage them when needed. You may want to follow up with some students later in the week. Be in prayer during this part of the discussion, asking God for wisdom as you facilitate.

5. See question four.

6. Have them read Jeremiah 1:4-5 again. Then have them think about what God has set them apart for. It may be wise to share some ideas from the Bible, such as holiness, obedience, sharing the gospel with others, serving others, worshiping God in spirit and

in truth, growing in knowledge and wisdom, and being a person of integrity. These things describe a person's character, rather than a future occupation. Let them know that God is more interested in who they'll be than *what* they'll be.

7. Give them a moment to think about this one. Then let them share their answer with the group. Be wise about what kind of commentary is necessary in response to their answers. Sometimes it's best just to let their answers hang in the air.

8. This is a deep question. However, challenge your students to think deeply about the significance of it. Basically, if God knows all about who we are and how our lives will unfold, that should be an incentive for us to fully trust God and worship him not only with our lips, but also our lives. The best thing we can do in response to this truth is seek to be the person God desires for us to be.

THE CLOSE

Give each person an index card and ask them to write their name and one thing they know God wants them to start doing this week. Have them give you their cards and commit to pray for each of them by name this week.

MORE
• **Instead of passing out index cards, have your group text you their name and answer. Then text them back throughout the week, letting them know you've been praying for them about that particular task.**
• **Make the celebrity montage activity into a game by sharing a couple of facts about each person first. See who can correctly identify the person before you finally show the picture as a last resort. This will help drive home the point that some in your group know more about a person's life than just being able to identify him or her in a picture.**
• **Make it your goal to have dinner with every person in your group (in parties of four). Do this to build a stronger sense of community in your group as you get to know your students better and help them get to know each other better, too.**

1. One thing that would make me throw up if I ever tasted it is…

SPITTING CONTEST

2. When I feel sick to my stomach, all I want is…

3. List some things that might make Jesus sick to his stomach.

4. Check out Revelation 3:15-16. What does Jesus have to say about spitting?

5. On a scale of 1 to 10 (with 1 being ice-cold and 10 being red-hot), how would you rate your commitment to Jesus by the way you live your life?

6. Do you think your life tastes good or bad in God's mouth? Why?

7. What needs to change in order for your life to be more savory in God's mouth?

8. When it comes to the way my life tastes to God, this week I'm going to…

THIS WEEK

In Revelation 3:15-16 Jesus addressed some people regarding the flavor and temperature (passion) of their lives. Your group will consider how their lives taste to God: Good or bad, savory or dry, hot or cold or even lukewarm.

OPENER

Start this session with an old-fashioned sunflower- or watermelon-seed spitting contest. Find an open area and let your students start spitting. Use a tape measure to see how far they can spit their seeds. If you're into cleanliness, go with the sunflower seeds. If you want it a bit more on the messy side, crack open a watermelon and enjoy a sticky-but-tasty time. After a winner is declared, start with question one.

THE DISCUSSION, BY NUMBERS

1. Have students finish the sentence about one food that would make them throw up. You may want to give your answer first. After all have shared, move on to the next question.
2. This question might help your group connect with each other as they share some of the routines that comfort them when they feel sick, such as placing a cool, wet washcloth on their forehead, sipping ginger ale, curling up with a pillow, and so on. Share yours and then let them share theirs.
3. Now move the conversation from thinking about themselves to what might make Jesus sick to his stomach. Give them a moment to write their thoughts and then listen to their answers. Remind them that they aren't so much thinking about food, but about what goes on in people's lives. You may need to offer an example or two to get them rolling, such as poverty, hurting children, and so on.
4. Have them read Revelation 3:15-16 and write down what Jesus has to say about spitting. Lukewarm lives make Jesus sick to his stomach and put a bad taste in his mouth.
5. Students should now rate the temperature of their lives from 1 to 10 (with 1 being ice-cold and 10 being red-hot) in terms of their relationship and commitments to Jesus. Have them share their answers and why they chose that rating.

6. Let them answer this question about how they perceive their lives to taste in God's mouth: Good or bad. Then let them give the reasons for their choice. You may want to expand this question and ask them about a time when they thought their lives tasted the best and the worst.
7. Have them think more deeply about their own lives and what needs to happen in order for their lives to taste more savory in God's mouth. After they have their answers, let them share with the group. Remind them that God loves us unconditionally. We can't do anything to earn God's love. However, the things we do affect the amount of pleasure we bring to God (based on our obedience to him).
8. Have them fill in the end of the sentence with an action step they'll take this week to make their lives taste better. You may need to give your answer first, such as by helping your neighbor with yard work, picking up the house without being asked, or writing a letter of encouragement to someone. Or you may have a bad habit that you want to change, such as watching less TV and each day investing 30 minutes to prayer and reading the Bible or listening to worship music and praising God.

THE CLOSE

As the students leave, give each one a sunflower or watermelon seed to remind them to live lives that won't make Jesus want to spit them out of his mouth. Tell them to stick the seed in their pocket and take it with them all week as a reminder to live tasty lives before God.

MORE

• Get your group to tell stories about the worst stomachaches they can remember and what caused them.
• Have your group pair off and have a contest to see how many different terms they can come up with for *throwing up* (*vomit, puke, upchuck, toss your cookies,* and so on).
• Have a watermelon-eating contest to see who can eat the most watermelon and who can extract the most seeds without using their fingers.

1. List several characteristics of a true friend.

2. What are the top three traits of a true friend?

3. The best thing about having a true friend is…

4. The hardest thing about *being* a true friend is…

5. Describe a time when a friend stabbed you in the back.

6. Oscar Wilde said, "True friends stab you in the front." What do you think he meant by this statement?

7. Write out Proverbs 27:6. What do you think this verse means in response to the quote in question six?

8. Describe a situation when you should be a true friend and "stab someone in the front."

9. Has someone ever stabbed you in the front? If so, how did it affect your relationship?

10. To whom do you need to give permission to stab you in the front?

FRIENDS: BACKSTABBER OR FRONT-STABBER?

17. FRIENDS: BACKSTABBER OR FRONT-STABBER?—Being a true friend and sharing the hard truth *(Proverbs 27:6)*

THIS WEEK
This TalkSheet will lead your group to talk about the characteristics of a true friend. Proverbs 27:6 says, "Wounds from a friend can be trusted." Another translation says, "Faithful are the wounds of a friend" (NKJV). True friends tell you the truth because they'd rather bruise you now than watch you bleed later.

OPENER
Start by showing the opening scene from an episode of *Friends*—just the "I'll Be There for You" theme song and montage—to get your group in the mood to talk about friends. You may also want to ask your students about their favorite television shows or movies that portray friendships. Get them talking and then move on to the TalkSheet questions.

THE DISCUSSION, BY NUMBERS
1. Have your group write down all the traits and characteristics of a true friend. After a few minutes, let them take turns sharing with the group. Record their answers on a whiteboard so these traits will stay before your group throughout the discussion.
2. Out of all the traits that were listed, have each person choose their top three traits of a true friend. Let the students share them with each other. You may want to keep tabs on what's shared to see if there's an overwhelming trait that surfaces.
3. Let your group answer questions three and four before sharing what they wrote to complete both sentences. There are no right or wrong answers. However, you may learn quite a bit about what's going on with your group as you listen.
4. See question three.
5. Ask for volunteers to share about an experience when a friend stabbed them in the back. What was the situation and how did it turn out?
6. Have them consider the statement: "True friends stab you in the front." Let them wrestle with it a bit and be sure to keep the discussion on track. Middle school guys are notorious for derailing conversations when phrases can be taken the wrong way. If they don't get it, don't give it away just yet. Let them move on to the next question and give them some time to process the two together.

7. Have them write out Proverbs 27:6 and what they think the verse means in light of the quote in question six. (It's about telling people the truth about issues that need to be dealt with in their lives.)
8. Ask them to describe some situations in which a person would need to be a true friend and "stab someone in the front." For example, when a friend considers experimenting with drugs, you'd talk with him about how dangerous it is, rather than not say anything.
9. Ask your group to talk about a time in their own lives when someone "stabbed them in the front." Ask them how it made them feel and what the end result was.
10. Sometimes the most difficult thing about telling someone the hard truth is being unsure of how that person will receive it. If we're true friends, we shouldn't be afraid. One way to get over that fear is to give your friends permission to "stab you in the front." Ask your students to write down the names of people to whom they'll give permission to do that whenever necessary.

THE CLOSE
Challenge your group to talk with the person(s) they listed in question 10. Ask them to commit to have a true-friend discussion by the end of the week.

MORE
• **Put a small blob of mustard on the side of your mouth and pretend you don't know it's there. As your group comes in, see how many students don't say anything to you about it and how many tell you there's something on your face. This can be a simple experiment to help them see that true friends love you too much to let you walk around with mustard on your face.**
• **Have a parent or older teenager share a story about a time when someone should have "stabbed her in the front" about some destructive decisions she was making in her life.**
• **Put up a dartboard and play a game of nerf darts as you make the transition to talking about "stabbing someone in the front" or "hitting the bull's-eye" with the darts. Where are those places we need to aim for when dangerous or destructive choices are being made? Don't beat around the bush. Aim right for the bull's-eye and be willing to "shoot straight" with your friend out of a heart of compassion, gentleness, and love.**

REAL OR COUNTERFEIT?

1. How can a person determine if something is real or a counterfeit?

2. Why do people settle for a counterfeit when the real deal is available?

3. What determines whether a person is real or counterfeit?

4. What characteristics describe a real disciple of Jesus?

5. Check out John 8:31 and write down what Jesus says is a characteristic of someone who is a real disciple. What does Jesus mean?

6. What does Jesus say is the end result for his disciples who are real? (Check out John 8:32.)

7. How might knowing "the truth" help a person guard against becoming a counterfeit?

8. How can you and your friends accomplish what Jesus talks about in verse 31?

THIS WEEK

One trait that teenagers value is for people to be real and authentic. Jesus desires real followers as well. This TalkSheet will take your group through one indicator of how Jesus identifies those who are really his disciples and those who may just be faking it.

OPENER

Plan to have a few items on hand—both real and counterfeit—for the students to compare: Purses, clothes, money, musical instruments, sunglasses, and so on. (If a store knows you're using an item as part of an object lesson, they'll usually let you purchase it with the understanding that you'll return it the next day for a full refund.) Before the students arrive, place the items on a table and cover them with a sheet. Start the session by talking about counterfeit or imitation brands. On the backside of their TalkSheets, have your students make a list of five counterfeit items that people try to pass off as being real. After a few have shared their lists, ask if they've ever unknowingly purchased something that was counterfeit. Allow a few students to share their stories. Then remove the sheet and ask the students to guess which items are real and which are counterfeit.

THE DISCUSSION, BY NUMBERS

1. Some answers might include comparing them side by side, the product's sturdiness, how it fades after it's been washed, and so on. Beware of letting your kids handle any of the products on display. Many stores have a no-return policy for damaged or marked goods.

2. Let them discuss why people settle for counterfeit products. It will probably boil down to the cost of the real thing being too high. Hold on to this answer, as you may reference it again in question five. (Real disciples are willing to pay the price to be real followers of Jesus.)

3. Change the focus of the conversation from stuff to people. Ask them what they think about being labeled as real or counterfeit. Are these important labels? Why?

4. Now have them talk about the characteristics of a real follower of Jesus. Let them come up with these on their own without any hints or examples.

5. Jesus describes *real* disciples as those who hold to his teaching. Help them understand that Jesus desires for his disciples to be changed by the words of life in the Bible. Real disciples know God's Word and are more likely to know God's voice and God's will.

6. Let them answer this one by reading the next verse (8:32). The result of living by the Word of God is that "you will know the truth, and the truth will set you free."

7. Knowing the truth frees us from feeling as though we have to live a counterfeit life. Instead, we can begin to be who God desires us to be. Before you share this idea with your students, let them grapple with the question and see if they come up with something similar or even more insightful.

8. This is where they need to figure out how to apply what it means to "hold to [Jesus'] teaching." This goes beyond having a quiet time. It means memorizing and internalizing Scripture. However, it's hard to do that if we don't read the Bible to begin with. Let them come up with their own ideas for how they'll choose to do that this week and share them with the group.

THE CLOSE

Have a "disposable" New Testament on hand—one from which you can tear out the pages and give them to your students. After you've discussed question nine, rip out a page of the Bible and say, **If you took just this one page and read it every day this week, took it everywhere you went, meditated on it, even memorized it, then it would begin to change your life.** Now offer the page to a student who will commit to do that. Rip out and distribute another page and keep doing so until everyone has one. Challenge them to bring their pages back the next time and share what happened. (Run this idea by your lead pastor before you do it—just so your supervisor understands that you aren't desecrating the Bible in a thoughtless manner.)

MORE

• **Wear fake brand-name clothes as a visual reminder that although your clothes might be counterfeit, you cannot afford to be counterfeit as a person.**

• **Wear a bad toupee as you lead this discussion to demonstrate how obvious and ridiculous it is not to be yourself.**

1. In what classes do you feel like you're listening to Charlie Brown's teacher?

SELECTIVE HEARING

2. When do you feel like your parents are talking to you like Charlie Brown's teacher?

3. Besides at school and with your parents, in what other situations do you feel like you're listening to Charlie Brown's teacher?

4. Why do you think the above situations make it difficult for you to listen and focus on what's being said?

5. Check out 1 Samuel 3:1-10. How did Samuel respond when God called his name?

6. Look at verse 10 again. If God called your name tonight, what do you think he'd want to say to you?

7. If you could ask God three questions and he would give you the answers, what would your three questions be?

8. How can you really know if God is speaking to you?

THIS WEEK

One of the great challenges for middle schoolers is to avoid tuning out adults. It's also difficult for them to hear God's voice, yet God still desires to speak to them. This TalkSheet is designed to help your group members think about the challenges they face when listening to people in authority, as well as to God.

OPENER

Start by asking if they've ever had trouble focusing on what their teachers are saying. Ahead of time, Google "Charlie Brown's teacher" and look for audio files that your group can listen to. Or get one of the Charlie Brown specials on DVD, one that shows the characters listening to their teacher in class. It's important that your group be able to listen to the sound the teacher makes so they can connect with what you're talking about.

THE DISCUSSION, BY NUMBERS

1. Let them talk about times in class when it felt like they were listening to Charlie Brown's teacher. Invest some time in this one to make sure your group is on board with you for the rest of the discussion.

2. Now move from the classroom to their homes. Get them talking about their relationships with their parents. The object is to have your students talk about specific situations when they felt as though their parents were talking on and on, but they'd checked out mentally.

3. Challenge them to think a bit here, since teachers and parents are the two easiest examples for them to relate to. It may be helpful to give them an example from your own life. Perhaps it's when you're at work or listening to a neighbor or relative who just talks and talks. The goal is to have your students connect with the concept of not really hearing what someone is saying.

4. This is an opinion question, so they can't be wrong. Encourage them to be honest with their answers. They may throw out A.D.D. or A.D.H.D. as an answer, or maybe they just get bored with people. Whatever they say, listen and encourage them in their honesty.

5. Have them read 1 Samuel 3:1-10 and answer the question before discussing it. Basically, Samuel kept hearing God talking to him, and he did his best to respond with an attentive attitude. Three times he went to his master, Eli, whom he thought was calling him. And then the last time God called, Samuel took his mentor's advice and prayed a simple prayer: "Speak, for your servant is listening."

6. Have your students reread verse 10 and write down what they think God would say to them. Encourage them to be honest. After they've had a moment to process their answer, listen to their responses. You may want to go first to set the tone on this question.

7. Give your group a few minutes to think and write down their three questions for God. Challenge them to think deeper on this one. Ask them to share their responses with the rest of the group.

8. Allow your students to share their thoughts before you clarify the answer from church history. Although there are various answers to this question, the ones that are normally accepted are (1) The words of the Bible: "Those who hear God's voice the most know his Word the best." God will never say anything that contradicts the Bible. (2) Wisdom from trusted and mature followers of Christ. (3) Circumstances in life. (4) Personal experiences with God and others, such as prayer, meditation, or other life experiences that don't contradict the Bible.

THE CLOSE

Challenge your group to take five minutes each day to simply pray: "Speak, for your servant is listening"—and then listen.

MORE

• Watch *Bruce Almighty* and *Evan Almighty* and then talk about the ways the characters heard from God.

• Let your group make up their own Charlie Brown's teacher voice tracks and download them as ringtones on their cell phones. There's even software you can purchase that alters a person's voice to sound like Charlie Brown's teacher.

• Write down everything you think God might be saying to you during your five minutes of listening to God each day (see The Close) and share it with a friend or the group next week.

FREEZE FRAME

1. If I were to snap a picture of love, it would look like…

2. If someone were to snap a picture of Jesus, it would communicate…

3. If someone were to snap a picture of my life, it would communicate…

4. "As a follower of Jesus, everything I do gives a picture of who Jesus is to a watching world." What do you think this statement means?

5. Check out 2 Corinthians 5:20. What do you think being an ambassador of Christ might have to do with living a life that gives accurate pictures of who Jesus is?

6. A person I know whose life is giving great pictures of who Jesus is, is…

7. When it comes to my life, the pictures that look the most like Jesus are…

But the pictures that need to look more like Jesus are…

THIS WEEK

Ralph Waldo Emerson said, "What you are speaks so loudly that I cannot hear what you are saying." The Bible describes followers of Jesus as his ambassadors, which means our lives should display a picture of what Jesus is about. This TalkSheet will focus on the kinds of pictures our lives display.

OPENER

Divide your group into teams and equip each with a digital camera. Take your students to a mall or other area where there are lots of people and images to capture. Then allow the teams 30 minutes to an hour to take a variety of interesting pictures. Make it a contest to see who can capture pictures that best depict certain themes, such as peace, love, or joy. Or turn them loose and tell them to come back with 10 interesting pictures at a designated time. Set it up so the teams can download their pictures onto a computer and then project them onto a screen for the whole group to see. (Consider playing the song "Freeze-Frame" by The J. Geils Band as you view the pictures.) After all the groups have returned, a panel of judges should choose the best in each category. When you're ready to move on to the TalkSheet, tell the group to answer the first question.

THE DISCUSSION, BY NUMBERS

1. You may need to give an example to get them started. If you were to capture a picture of "love," you might photograph the moment when the bride and groom share that first kiss. Give a few examples that depict expressions of "love" and encourage them to get creative in thinking about the places and situations where they might capture the perfect picture of "love."

2. If a picture is worth a thousand words, what would a picture of Jesus communicate? Let them think about this and consider what Jesus would be doing in the picture. Be cautious about giving examples so you don't taint their thinking. Don't be afraid to probe a bit as you encourage them to think deeper.

3. Now challenge your group to think about what messages would be conveyed in photos of their own lives. Depending on how well your group

knows one another, you may want to ask others in the group to offer their ideas.

4. Let your group process this concept together. If it's true, what kinds of pictures of Jesus are their friends looking at when they look at their lives?

5. Have your group turn to 2 Corinthians 5:20 and ask one student to read it out loud. Ask what an "ambassador" is supposed to be. (Someone who represents another person as if that other person were present.) Based on this definition, what does it mean to be an ambassador, and what does it have to do with giving accurate pictures of Jesus to a watching world? (If we're followers of Jesus, we're to live lives that look like, walk like, talk like, respond like, and approach life just like Jesus would.)

6. You may want to offer your example first, but let them name someone whose life gives great pictures of Jesus. Ask why they selected that person.

7. Have them fill in the two blanks by indicating one area in which they feel as though they're giving accurate pictures, as well as an area in which they believe they need to do some work before it will look like Jesus.

THE CLOSE

Challenge your group to snap pictures of people or things that communicate the love and life of Jesus in the coming week. Ask them to email these pictures to one another as a reminder to live lives that show great pictures of who Jesus is.

MORE

• **Every week for a month, select a different theme that describes an attribute of Jesus, such as joy, love, peace, strength, compassion, patience, kindness, and focus, and ask your group to capture pictures that depict that theme.**

• **Create a common space where your group can post their pictures and add to them in the days ahead. It could be a physical place (such as a bulletin board) where your group meets or someplace online, such as a MySpace, Facebook, or Flickr account.**

• **Challenge your group to invite friends who may not be followers of Jesus to participate in the photo project as a creative way to begin new conversations with them.**

OPEN OR SHUT?

1. Describe a time when your parents told you to do something and you didn't do it. What was the result?

2. Describe a time when you did something without your parents having to tell you to do it. What was the result? How did they react?

3. Why do you think keeping the doors closed is such a big deal to parents?

4. Check out what Jesus says in Matthew 23:13-14. Who was Jesus talking to in this verse and what was he accusing them of doing?

5. Why was Jesus so angry at these people?

6. Describe a time when you felt like the door was shut in your face.

7. Describe a time when you may have shut the door in someone's face.

8. Based on what Jesus was talking about in the verse mentioned above, what do you think it looks like to open the door to the kingdom for someone?

9. Who has opened the door of the kingdom for you?

10. Who might God want you to open the door of the kingdom for this week?

THIS WEEK

Perhaps your students have felt as though the door of the kingdom has been shut in their faces before. Or maybe they've shut the door in someone else's face. This discussion will take the common metaphor of a door and connect it to a powerful teaching of Jesus.

OPENER

Start the discussion near a refrigerator and have your students gather around it as you share how you often heard your parents remind you to "Shut the door! You're letting the cold out." Perhaps it wasn't just the refrigerator door. They could be referring to the back door or the front door in the middle of summer when the air conditioner was running. Chances are good that your group can relate to this experience. After you've made your point and found a connection with your group regarding the command to "shut the door," have your group move on to the TalkSheet questions.

THE DISCUSSION, BY NUMBERS

1. Now it's time for your students to share some personal stories about when their parents told them not to do something and they chose to do it anyway. What was the outcome and the reactions or consequences?

2. Now shift the focus of the conversation a bit. Have your students share about a time when they did something for their parents—a chore or some other deed—without their parents having to ask them. What was their parents' reaction and how did it play out?

3. Now that you have them talking a bit, go back to the illustration of the doors. This question is intended to segue into what Jesus says to a group of religious people who were shutting the door in people's faces.

4. Have your group read Matthew 23:13-14. Jesus was accusing the religious leaders of making it hard for people to come into a relationship with God and enter into the kingdom. Thus, he accused them of shutting the door of the kingdom in people's faces.

5. Let your group members wrestle with this question a bit. Jesus consistently seems agitated and angry with the religious people of the day because they weighed people down with unnecessary religious rules.

6. Ask your group to share a time when they felt like a door of some kind was shut in their faces. Remind them that this isn't a literal door. Rather, what metaphorical door has been shut in their face? Not all of the students may be able to share in this question. Ask those who can to describe how they felt.

7. Now flip the question about the door. Have them share about a time when they shut the door in someone else's face. Encourage them to be honest and open. If appropriate, probe a bit on their answers. Why did they do it? How did it make them feel? How did it affect their relationship with that person?

8. Challenge your group to think deeply about this question. Rather than give your opinions, let them wrestle with this one for a bit.

9. Ask them each to name a person who "opened the door of the kingdom" to them. If they had trouble answering the previous question, ask them to consider the reasons why they chose the person they did for this question. What characteristics and actions led them to select this person?

10. Ask them each to write the initials of the person they believe God wants them to open the door of the kingdom for this week.

THE CLOSE

Challenge your group to write the person's initials from question 10 on a sticky note and place it on the door of their bedroom as a reminder to be praying and intentionally seeking ways to open the door of the kingdom for that person.

MORE

• **Encourage your students to be intentional about holding doors open for people this week—and also to let it be a reminder about opening the door of heaven to others, too.**

• **Buy a door at a local hardware store and let your group write or paint the initials of the people they thought of for question 10 on the door.**

• **Challenge your students so that each time they walk through a door during the coming week, they should whisper a prayer for their friends who need to enter a relationship with Jesus and his kingdom.**

BUT EVERYBODY ELSE IS DOING IT!

1. What does everybody else get to do that you wish your parents would let you do, too?

2. Why won't your parents let you do it?

3. What's something your parents wouldn't let you do when you were younger, but now they do? Was it as fun or fulfilling as you thought it would be?

4. When it comes to peer pressure, what three things are your friends most tempted to do?

5. Check out Micah 4:5. What was "everybody else doing" that the people of God were not going to do—no matter what?

6. Why do you believe the answer to question five is or isn't a big deal to God?

7. What does it mean for someone to "walk in the name of Lord"?

8. What's the one thing that you know will make God happy if you don't do it, but it's also the hardest thing for you not to do because everybody else is doing it?

9. What's the one thing that you know will make God happy if you do it, but it's the hardest thing for you to do because nobody else is doing it?

THIS WEEK

For generations one of the echoing phrases from the mouths of teenagers has been "But everyone else is doing it." This TalkSheet will look at how God desires for his followers to keep following him and walking in his name regardless of what everybody else is doing.

OPENER

Begin this session by polling how many students in your group have said something like, "But everybody else is doing it," to their parents, only to have them reply with, "Well, if everyone was jumping off a building, would that make it right?" The object here is simply to get everybody on the same page and feeling as though they aren't the only ones who've had a conversation with their parents about something they wanted to do but weren't allowed to. Once you feel as though they're tracking with you, move forward by having them answer the TalkSheet questions.

THE DISCUSSION, BY NUMBERS

1. Have your group get specific about the things their parents won't let them do that everybody else gets to do. You may want to break the ice and talk about the things you weren't allowed to do in middle school.
2. Have them discuss why their parents won't allow them to do whatever they wish.
3. Your group should come to the consensus that what they thought was such a big deal when they were children isn't really that big of a deal now that they're older.
4. Talk about the issue of peer pressure. Have your group list the top three things they believe "everybody else is doing" but they aren't allowed to do.
5. Make the point that peer pressure has been around for ages. Have your group look up Micah 4:5 and talk about what "everybody else" was doing that God's followers were not going to do. (They were following other gods.)
6. Let your group members talk about why God thought this was a big deal. (God is a jealous God who desires people to worship and follow only him. Cf. Exodus 20:3-5.)
7. Have your group talk through what they believe it means to "walk in the name of the Lord." (i.e., Making

choices in every area of our lives that honor God and bring him glory regardless of what we're doing or where we are at the time.)
8. Ask your group to complete their answers to questions eight and nine before sharing them with the group. Encourage them to be honest with their answers, rather than just giving the answer they believe everyone else wants to hear. You may want to give your own answers first to set the tone.
9. See question eight.

THE CLOSE

Challenge your group to send each other simple text messages that let each other know they aren't alone in their choices to live for God and walk in his name. Have them send a message such as UR NOT WALKING ALONE 2DAY. Let them make up their own messages that they'll commit to send to each other until the group gets back together next week.

MORE

• **Challenge your group to start a new trend or fad of some sort just to see if "everybody else" will do it, too. Let them make up the new trend or fad as a group. Maybe they'll begin using a new word or phrase. Maybe they'll start a new hobby and see how many other people they can get to do it with them.**
• **Show your group the clip from *Can't Buy Me Love* when Ronald Miller (played by Patrick Dempsey) learns how to dance by mistakenly watching The African Anteater Ritual dance on PBS' African Cultural Hour. When he goes to the school dance, he starts doing his new moves by himself. But before long, everyone else is doing the new "dance" as well. Have your group discuss what this scene represents when it comes to peer pressure and the phrase "everybody else is doing it."**
• **Challenge your group to blatantly go against the flow and not do what "everybody else is doing." Have your group determine what those things are and make a pact not to do them for a week as their own subtle, yet intentional, commitment to live a life that goes against the flow.**

1. In what subject would you say you have the best shot at being a know-it-all?

2. In what subject would your friends say you're a know-it-all?

3. What would you do if you really *did* know it all?

4. Look at John 13:3. What does that verse say about Jesus?

5. In John 13:4-5, how did Jesus choose to act even though he "knew it all" and had all power under his God-given authority?

6. Why did Jesus respond to his disciples that way? (See John 13:12-16 for some hints.)

7. As you begin to know more about what Jesus expects of his followers, what does he want you to do in response to this new knowledge? (See John 13:17.)

8. What are some things Jesus wants you to do with your life today—this week, this month, this year—to follow his example?

THIS WEEK

This TalkSheet allows for your students to look at the life of Jesus and figure out how they can follow his example of humble servant-leadership even when they may know or understand more than the people around them do.

OPENER

Start your group time with an old-fashioned trivia game to see who will be crowned the group's Know-It-All. There are lots of trivia-game sites online. Google "teen trivia games" to find a few you can use. (At the time of this writing, one site that offered several options was *http://teentrivia.student.com/.*) Have some fun with the game and get the whole group involved. Divide your group into teams and then ask a series of questions. Have all of the teams (or individuals) guess before you share the right answers. After you've finished with the trivia game, have your students take a look at their TalkSheets.

THE DISCUSSION, BY NUMBERS

1. Tell your group that the trivia champion won because they happened to know a little bit more than everyone else. Ask them to identify the one subject they believe they know the most about—something that if all the questions were about that particular subject, then they'd win the trivia game hands-down.

2. Now have your group answer the same question, except have them answer according to what they believe their friends would say.

3. Ask your group to consider what they'd do if they were omniscient—knowing all things. Encourage them to be creative in their answers.

4. Have your group look up John 13:3. This verse is saying that Jesus was fully aware that God the Father had put all things under his power. In other words, Jesus knew all things completely and had the power and authority from God to exercise that power and knowledge if he chose to do so.

5. Now have your group read the next two verses, John 13:4-5. Have them talk about Jesus' response to being a know-it-all who had all power. What do they think about his response—washing the feet of his followers and friends? Such an act was one of

utter humility and normally done by the hired help. It certainly wasn't customary for a leader to wash anyone's feet.

6. Ask your group to talk about the possible reasons why Jesus—the most powerful person on earth who also knew everything—performed such an act of humility. John 13:12-16 indicates that Jesus was setting an example for his disciples to follow. Jesus demonstrated how true leaders should act. They should be humble and serve others in love.

7. You'll unpack this idea some more during the next question. But basically Jesus desires people to act on what they know to be right and true, rather than simply gaining more head knowledge or useless trivia that has no impact in their lives.

8. Ask your students to talk about some of the things they've learned recently about what Jesus wants them to do. It could be things you've talked about with them in recent gatherings or lessons they've learned and remembered over the course of their lives. Regardless, the question is intended to point them back to what Jesus says to his followers in John 13:17. They're to act on what they now know. Simply being a know-it-all is no good in Jesus' eyes if people don't act on what they know.

THE CLOSE

Have your group members write down this quote from John Maxwell: "I contend that we are educated as Christians way beyond our level of obedience." Ask your students to think about the quote as they leave. Then suggest that they email or text you what they think it means in relation to today's discussion. Pray for your group and then dismiss them.

MORE
- **Arrange to have your group wash each other's feet.**
- **Instead of a trivia contest, your group could participate in an old-fashioned spelling bee to generate some friendly competition.**

NICKNAMES

1. What are the top three coolest nicknames you've heard?

2. What are the top three lamest nicknames you've heard?

3. How did one of your friends get his nickname?

4. Check out the following verses and write the nicknames Jesus gave some of his friends:

   • Mark 3:16—Simon was now _____.

   • Mark 3:17—James and John, the sons of Zebedee, were now _____
     or _____.

   • Mark 3:18—another guy named Simon was known as _____.

5. What was the reason for these guys' nicknames?

   • Simon

   • James and John

   • Simon

6. Now check out John 13:23 and write down what another one of Jesus' friends was known as.

7. How do you think people would describe you if you were the one being spoken of in John 13:23? What nickname would they give you?

8. Check out Revelation 2:17. What nickname will Jesus give to you one day?

THIS WEEK

The TalkSheet is designed to show a side of Jesus that your students may not have noticed before. Jesus connected with some of his close friends by giving them nicknames. Sometimes it's easy to forget how real the God of the universe was when he walked on earth.

OPENER

Start by telling your group not too many people are known by only their first names. Throw out a couple of examples, such as Elvis and Madonna, and then let your group come up with as many additional examples as they can. After your group has exhausted their list, have them move on to the TalkSheet.

THE DISCUSSION, BY NUMBERS

1. After your students have had a chance to choose their top-three coolest nicknames, have them share their answers with the group.
2. Now have them write their top-three lamest nicknames. Have some fun with this and feel free share your own list and why you think the names are so lame.
3. Oftentimes, nicknames are given to people due to a story or something they did that caused a nickname to "stick." Have your group write the name of someone they know who has such a nickname and then ask a few of them to share the story behind it.
4. Have your group read Mark 3:13-19 (about the calling of the 12 disciples) and write down the nicknames of three of Jesus' disciples.
• Mark 3:16—Simon was nicknamed "Peter."
• Mark 3:17—James and John, the sons of Zebedee, were nicknamed *Boanerges*—or "sons of thunder."
• Mark 3:18—another guy named Simon was known as "the Zealot."
5. Ask your group to discuss why Jesus gave the men these particular nicknames. The name *Peter* means "rock." In a sense, Jesus saw Simon as a literal rock—one who was solid and hard-nosed, someone he could build his church upon. Perhaps the "sons of thunder" spoke with boldness and power. Simon the Zealot had a radical nature and a flair for being all-or-nothing when it came to his political views and anti-Rome stance.
6. In John 13:23, John is referred to as "the disciple whom Jesus loved." Some have also referred to John as "the beloved." This was a term of endearment in

that day and one that described the affection Jesus had for his dear friend John.
7. Let your group have a little fun with this. The other disciples at the Last Supper referred to John as "the disciple whom Jesus loved." Have your group imagine they're sitting in John's place. What do they think the other disciples would have known about them in the retelling of the story? Again, it may be something out of the story of your students' lives or some characteristic they exhibit on a regular basis. You may want to go first on this one. How would the disciples have described you and your relationship with Jesus?
8. Have your group read Revelation 2:17. Some scholars believe this verse talks about a literal new name that each follower of Jesus will receive in the last day. For those who overcome and persevere to the end, this nickname from Jesus will be a special term of endearment that will most likely come forth from the story of that person's life. If this is the case, what nickname might be written on your stone? Let your group ponder this question before sharing what they hope their new nicknames will be. Allow them to offer suggestions for Jesus' nicknames for other group members as well.

THE CLOSE

Give each student a small river rock (you can get them from the landscaping section at Lowe's) and a Sharpie marker and have them write the nickname they hope Jesus will one day give to them. They don't need to share this nickname with anyone. However, suggest that your students take the rocks home with them as a reminder of their desired name.

MORE

• **At the beginning of the session, give each student a nickname. Everyone in the group must then refer to each other by their nicknames during the course of the day.**
• **Challenge your group to address each other throughout the week by their preferred nicknames as a way to remember the discussion.**
• **Remind your group of the significance of names in the Bible. Then challenge them to go to a bookstore or library with Christian resources and look up the meanings of some of the names in the Bible. Have them report their findings to the group the following week.**

1. What's the most valuable thing you own? Why?

2. What's the most valuable thing you do all week?

3. It's been said you'll either add value to people and lift them up, or you'll subtract value from people and beat them down. Do you agree or disagree? Why?

4 Check out the following passages and determine how Jesus added value to people.

- Matthew 4:23-25

- Matthew 8:1-3

- Matthew 9:1-8

- Matthew 9:9-13

- Matthew 9:18-26

- Matthew 14:13-21

- Matthew 28:18-20

5. What's one way Jesus has added value to your life?

6. What's one way you can add value to someone's life this week?

THIS WEEK

This week's discussion revolves around the concept of adding value to the lives of others. Everywhere Jesus went, he added value to the lives of those he came in contact with. This TalkSheet will allow your group to look at various accounts in the Gospel of Matthew and see how Jesus did this.

OPENER

The Price Is Right has a game called "1 Right Price" during which contestants must choose which item is worth the displayed dollar amount. Create your own game by using either real objects or pictures of them. Play 10 rounds with two items in each round. Show the actual price of one item, and then have your students guess which object is worth that amount. Students should keep track of their correct guesses on the backs of their TalkSheets. After the game have your group talk about what determines something's value before moving on to the TalkSheet.

THE DISCUSSION, BY NUMBERS

1. Have your group consider their possessions and write down the one thing they value most. When they share with the group, make sure they explain why the item is so valuable.

2. Now shift their perspective of *value* and have them consider the most valuable thing they *do*. Feel free to give your own examples.

3. There's no right or wrong answer to this one. Ask your students to share the reasoning behind their answers.

4. Ask a different student to look up each passage. Tell your group that Jesus consistently added value to people's lives. Before the passages are read aloud, ask your students to listen for ways that Jesus added value to people.

- Matthew 4:23-25—Jesus taught, proclaimed the Good News, and healed people.
- Matthew 8:1-3—Jesus healed a man with leprosy and even touched him—a social outcast.
- Matthew 9:1-8—Jesus forgave sin, asked good questions, healed a paralyzed man and affirmed the faith of this man's friends.

- Matthew 9:9-13—Jesus called a tax collector (another social outcast) to follow him and then ate dinner at his home.
- Matthew 9:18-26—Jesus listened to people's requests, healed and encouraged a woman, and healed a little girl.
- Matthew 14:13-21—Jesus had compassion on the crowds, healed the sick, taught his disciples, and fed the multitudes.
- Matthew 28:18-20—Jesus gave his followers purpose for their lives and assured them that he'd always be with them.

5. Have your group share the ways Jesus has added value to their lives.

6. Wrap up the discussion by having your group consider one way they can add value to someone else's life during the coming week.

THE CLOSE

Give each student a printed version of the quote from question four: YOU'LL EITHER ADD VALUE TO PEOPLE AND LIFT THEM UP OR YOU'LL SUBTRACT VALUE FROM PEOPLE AND BEAT THEM DOWN. WHICH ONE WILL YOU DO TODAY? Challenge them to put it someplace where they'll see it each morning and consider which one they'll choose.

MORE

- **Invite an expert appraiser to share with your group. Interview the person and ask her to talk about what makes some things valuable and what decreases the value of other things.**
- **Ask students to keep track of how many times they add value and how many times they subtract value from someone during the week. Each time they add value (encouraging someone), they should give themselves a point. If they subtract value (criticizing or making fun of someone), they must subtract a point from their total. Compare scores the following week.**
- **Have your students write notes to people who've given value to them, thanking them for who they are and the value they've added to your students' lives. Then have them mail the notes as a way to encourage these people and add value to their lives in return.**

1. What dinner do your parents make that you never have trouble cleaning your plate?

2. What dinner do your parents make that you have the most trouble cleaning your plate?

3. The most food I've ever eaten in one sitting would have to be...

4. Check out Proverbs 21:20 and write it in the space provided. What do you think this verse means when it comes to cleaning your plate?

5. What do you think God is really trying to say in this verse?

6. Why might this message be important for your life?

7. What's one thing God might want you to do this week in response to this verse?

THIS WEEK

This TalkSheet centers on the importance of saving, rather than consuming everything all at once. Proverbs 21:20 speaks to the wisdom of setting aside choice foods and oils. In our consumeristic society, this lesson could be a real challenge for many students and adults.

OPENER

Start the session with an old-fashioned "clean your plate" contest. Any food of equal proportion will do. It might be easiest to have multiple contestants compete to see who can clean a pie tin full of whipped cream the fastest. Make it interesting and forbid them to use their hands. The first one to clean his or her plate is the champion. Segue to the TalkSheet by asking your students to talk about when their parents made them clean their plates.

THE DISCUSSION, BY NUMBERS

1. Have your group share about the meals they love so much that they never have a problem cleaning their plates.
2. Now have your students share about the meals they dislike so much that they really struggle to clean their plates.
3. Have your group members recall when they ate the most food in one sitting. Where were they and what did they eat?
4. Now have them read Proverbs 21:20 and write the verse in the space provided: "The wise store up choice food and oil, but fools gulp theirs down." Challenge your group to think deeper. Is there a concept that God wants people to understand? Let your group give their answers and then challenge them to consider that maybe God is encouraging people not to consume all they have in one sitting. Rather, it's wise to save some of what God has provided for you to use at a later date.
5. Being a person who saves will move me toward becoming a person who is wise. If all I do is "clean my plate" in the various areas of my life, in God's eyes I am acting like a foolish person.
6. This is an opinion question. Let your students wrestle with this one if they don't get it right off the bat. Even if there isn't much discussion, encourage them to think about their answer. Hesitate to give them your take on it. Sometimes it's healthy for people to walk away from a discussion on spiritual things without having all the answers spoon-fed to them.
7. Wrap up your discussion by having your group brainstorm some ideas of things they could do in response to this Proverb. Encourage them to begin incorporating one idea into their daily lives this week.

THE CLOSE

Challenge your group to make a commitment to leave a portion on their plate at each meal to serve as a reminder not to be foolish in "gulping theirs down." Suggest that they take home doggie bags if they're eating in a restaurant and save part of their meals for later as another way to remind themselves of Proverbs 21:20.

MORE

• **Have someone with a financial-planning background briefly share what saving a little bit at a time can become if people stay committed to saving. Obviously, middle schoolers don't make much money—if any. However, this could be an illustration that sticks with them regarding good principles for handling their finances in the future.**

• **Ask a representative from an organization like World Vision or Compassion International to speak to your group about people around the world who have very little. However, you may want to point out to your students that the same principle from Proverbs 21:20 applies whether a person has much or little.**

• **If you have access to the Internet, you can watch video footage of eating contests. "Cleaning your plate" has become a sport with quite a following. Google "eating contest" and see what you find. There are some great clips under "hot dog eating contest."**

1. What's the main difference between a candle and a light bulb?

THIS LITTLE LIGHT OF MINE

2. Check out Matthew 5:14-16. Do you think Jesus would rather you be more like a lit candle or a light bulb?

4. Describe a situation in which you might be tempted to be more like a light bulb.

5. What are the characteristics of a person whose light shines bright for Christ?

6. What are the characteristics of a person who believes in Jesus but is more like a light bulb than a candle that burns consistently in life?

7. Why would followers of Jesus ever want to hide their light?

9. Why do you think it's important that others glorify God when they see your good deeds, rather than praise you for living well?

10. What's one area of your life in which you feel like your light is shining the brightest?

11. What's one area of your life in which your light needs to shine brighter?

12. What do you think God wants you to do to make sure your light shines as bright as possible?

THIS WEEK

This TalkSheet will allow your group to discuss what it means to let your light shine so the world knows you belong to God. Imagine what would happen to the darkness if all who claimed to follow Jesus let the light of Christ shine through their lives.

OPENER

Before your group meets, turn off any overhead lights, cover the windows, and light the room with only a candle and a lamp without a shade (so its light bulb is exposed). As your students enter the room, give each of them a small votive candle (with a tin bottom for catching dripping wax) and have a leader light it as they find their places. Tell them not to blow out the candle, but hold onto it and keep it burning throughout the meeting. The ambiance of the room will hopefully set the tone for the discussion. Once everybody is seated, ask them to write down their answer to the first question on their TalkSheets.

THE DISCUSSION, BY NUMBERS

1. A lit candle cannot be turned off and on like a light bulb. When someone makes this point, turn the light bulb off and on for effect.
2. Have your group read Matthew 5:14-16. Ask whether they believe Jesus would prefer our lives to be more like a candle or a light bulb. Make sure they give reasons for their answers. Hopefully they'll say Jesus wants them be more like a lit candle because once it's lit, it has no choice but to burn bright.
3. Ask your group to talk about situations when they might be tempted to turn their faith off and on. You may need to give them an example, such as when they're around friends who aren't shining bright for Jesus and they're tempted to just fit in.
4. Talk about the characteristics of people whose lives burn bright for Jesus, such as honesty and humility.
5. Now have your group consider the characteristics of a person who believes in Jesus but whose life is more like a light bulb. A word that may come up is *hypocrite*.

6. After they've had a chance to share their thoughts, you might mention situations that take place in countries that are hostile to Christians, such as persecution and imprisonment.
7. Take a minute and have someone reread Matthew 5:16 where it talks about others glorifying God because they see your life shine with the light of Jesus. Hopefully your group will clue in to the fact that God desires for your life to point people toward God, rather than your own accomplishments.
8. Have your group focus on the brightest place in their lives. Use this question as an excuse to praise and encourage your students as they share their thoughts on where they're shining brightly.
9. Now have your group consider where they need to start burning brighter. Encourage your group to be honest and really consider the place that needs some serious growth.
10. Ask your students to zero in on an action step that will allow their lives to shine and make God look great. Once they suggest an area, ask them to commit to begin fulfilling it this week.

THE CLOSE

Encourage your group to take their candles home with them and use them as they pray and read Matthew 5:14-16 as a reminder of who God desires for them to be. Challenge them to memorize this passage. Close the time in prayer and have students blow out their candles before leaving your group meeting.

MORE
• Play "Shine" by the Newsboys as your students are entering and leaving your meeting space.
• At the beginning of your session, have a child sing "This Little Light of Mine" and let your students do the hand motions, if they know them. If your church has a children's choir, it's likely that they'll know this song, too.
• Give each student a votive candle when they exit as a way to remember that they're to be a light to others.

1. List the greatest movies or television shows about space.

2. The coolest thing about space is…

3. The scariest thing about space is…

DANGER!

4. What dangers have you been warned about in the past?

5. Check out 1 Corinthians 10:11 and write the verse below.

6. What four things does Paul warn the church of Corinth about in 1 Corinthians 10?

   • v. 7

   • v. 8

   • v. 9

   • v. 10

7. What warning is Paul giving the people in verse 12?

8. What does Paul say will happen, according to verse 13, when we're put in difficult situations or when temptation is present in our lives?

9. The biggest temptation in my life that God is warning me about is…

   The best way for me to avoid that temptation is to…

THIS WEEK

This TalkSheet will help your group talk about warnings that are intended to keep us from destructive temptations. God always provides a way out that will lead us to the right choice.

OPENER

Introduce your group to *Lost in Space*, a television show that first aired in 1965 and lasted three seasons. Share a brief synopsis of the storyline, which can be found at the Internet Movie Database and Wikipedia Web sites. Two of the main characters were a young boy named Will Robinson (played by Bill Mumy) and The Robot. (It would be great if you could show the group pictures of the show's cast.) The Robot would regularly warn Will and his family by saying things like, "DANGER! DANGER!" A collection of audio files of The Robot giving various warnings is available on *www.wavcentral.com/tv/lost_space.html*. Consider playing one or two of them for your group or showing clips from the DVDs. Tell your students that you'll be discussing warnings, but first you want to talk about other television shows and movies about space. At this point turn them toward their TalkSheets.

THE DISCUSSION, BY NUMBERS

1. Get them talking by having them come up with their favorite television shows or movies about space.
2. Have them complete questions two and three before letting each person share their answers for the coolest thing about space.
3. Now let them share the scariest thing about space.
4. Tell your group that you want to go back to The Robot's words for a moment: "DANGER! DANGER!" What have adults warned them about in the past—this could be anything from staying away from drugs to not hitting their brothers or sisters. Let them discuss this one for a few minutes.
5. Have them read 1 Corinthians 10:11 and write it on their TalkSheets. Ask them to tell you why it says, "these things…were written down." *(They were written down as warnings.)*
6. Now have them check out verses 7-10 and write what the warnings are about in each of these verses. Ask why Paul took the time to write down

these warnings, rather than just tell the people.
- v. 7 = Don't be idolaters.
- v. 8 = Don't commit sexual immorality.
- v. 9 = Don't test Christ.
- v. 10 = Don't grumble.

7. Now have your group look up verse 12 and write down the warning. ("So, if you think you are standing firm, be careful that you don't fall!") Why was this warning important enough to be recorded in the Bible?
8. Have them wrap up this biblical discussion by seeing what Paul says about temptations and what God will do when they're tempted. Basically, they'll never face something that's unique to them alone. All people face a variety of temptations, and with each one, God is always faithful to provide a way of escape—if we're willing to heed the warnings.
9. As you wrap up the discussion, have each person fill in the last sentence with their answers for what they believe is their biggest temptation right now and what they think their best God-given plan of escape might be. Encourage everyone to share their answers and feel free to share your own.

THE CLOSE

Have your group commit to flash each other the "warning reminder sign" (based on Mr. Spock's Vulcan greeting) in the coming the week. Formed by holding the pinky and ring fingers together yet apart from the other three fingers to form a V, it's a famous hand gesture from *Star Trek (www.tvacres.com/greetings_spock.htm)*. Used for group accountability, this gesture would remind your students to heed the warnings, avoid the temptations, and head toward the wise choices that God desires.

MORE

- **Play clips from your favorite space-themed shows, such as the opening scene from *Star Wars* or perhaps some scenes from *Star Trek*.**
- **Have a sleepover with your group and enjoy a Star Wars Trilogy watching party. Better yet, watch all six episodes, if you can find enough soft drinks and candy to keep your students up all night!**
- **Host a video-game tournament with a space theme. Ask your students for recommendations of the best space games to play.**

1. Is there anyone in your family tree who's famous or has a particularly interesting story?

WHO'S YOUR DADDY?

2. Who do you know with special privileges because of family relationships?

3. Check out what John the Baptist said to the crowds in Luke 3:7-9. What emotions is he feeling as he speaks to them? Why do you think he feels that way?

4. In verse 8 who did John accuse his audience of claiming as their "daddy"? Why do you think John thought this was a big deal?

5. What does John say they need to be doing instead? Why is that suggestion more important than a family relationship?

6. What was the big deal about Abraham? (See God's covenant with Abraham in Genesis 12, 15, and 17.)

7. What does John say God will do to trees (people's lives) that don't produce good fruit?

8. What kind of fruit is your life producing?

THIS WEEK

As your group explores the passage in this Talk-Sheet, you'll have an opportunity to communicate the gospel as you help them work through some of the misconceptions regarding how people can be in a right relationship with God for all eternity.

OPENER

Start by telling your group a bit of your family history. Briefly talk about your parents and grandparents and share a few interesting things about their lives and where they're from. You could even show them a visual of a family tree to help your group see the people you're related to and where they originated from. After you've shared a bit about your family's background, have your group begin thinking about their own heritage by answering the questions on their TalkSheets.

THE DISCUSSION, BY NUMBERS

1. Take a few moments and let your group share stories of any famous people they claim to be related to or any unique stories that might be a part of their family history.

2. Ask your group to talk about relationships that give them special privileges, such as a family member in a political office who can give them VIP access to restricted areas. Make the point that who we're related to can lead to great things in this life. However, the Gospel of Luke says our earthly relationships have no bearing on our access to eternity with God.

3. Have someone read Luke 3:7-9 out loud and with emotion. Then have the group discuss what John the Baptist might have been feeling and why. John was frustrated and irritated by the lies on which these people were mistakenly basing their right standing before God.

4. John the Baptist accused them of saying their daddy was Abraham—the "ultimate ancestor" in that day. Let your group talk about why John was so upset; don't give them the answer too soon. John wanted the crowds to understand that eternal life and favor with God aren't based on the people in your family tree.

5. John believed the people's lives should produce fruit that would show evidence of their repentance. This means that because of who God is and what God has done in them and for them, their lives should

demonstrate on the outside what took place on the inside when they decided to follow Christ. Help your group understand that if their relationship with God were based on their earthly families, then Jesus didn't need to come to earth, die, and rise again to put humans back into right relationship with God.

6. Have your group turn back with you to Genesis 12, 15, and 17, but just paraphrase what happened. God initiated a covenant with Abraham (who used to be called "Abram") and promised him that he would be a father of many people and nations. The Luke passage shows how Abraham's descendents were still banking on their heritage to make them right with God, rather than focusing on their lives and relationship before God.

7. Ask your group to look at Luke 3:9 to determine what John said God would do to those whose lives bear no good fruit: Chop them down like a tree.

8. Have your group do some self-inspection. What kind of fruit are they producing? Challenge them to be honest and think of some things they could do this week that would serve as a demonstration of their relationship with God the Father through Jesus.

THE CLOSE

Remind your group that the Bible says true life is all about Who you're related to as a follower of Jesus, rather than a follower (or relative) of someone on earth. When it comes to eternity, the real question isn't *Who is your earthly father?* but *Are you a child of God the Father?* Is your life showing evidence of that relationship? If some of your students have never received a new life in Jesus, talk with them about what it means to make that decision today.

MORE

• **Offer your group some different perspectives on family trees and where people come from by asking some older adults from your church to share their family lineage.**

• **If you have access to a local celebrity who's also a follower of Jesus, have that person share his story about how he came to follow Christ and how his status and privilege in society means little when it comes to eternity and salvation.**

• **Brainstorm with your group to make a list of actions or behaviors that demonstrate "good fruit" in the life of a Jesus follower.**

REBEL WITH A CAUSE

1. List the names of people or fictional characters who could be considered "rebels."

2. What makes someone a rebel?

3. What's the most rebellious thing any of your friends have ever done?

4. What's the most rebellious thing you've ever done?

5. Check out Mark 10:45 and write it below. What examples from Jesus' life could serve as evidence that he was the ultimate rebel with a cause?

6. Based on Jesus' definition of being a rebel, what's the most "rebellious" thing you could do?

7. Why don't more people choose to pattern their lives after Jesus?

8. If you chose to pattern your life after the rebellious example of Jesus, what would be the most difficult thing for you?

9. What would be the biggest benefits if you chose to be a rebel like Jesus?

THIS WEEK

If rebellion means "going against the flow of society," a case can be made that the greatest rebel ever to walk the earth was Jesus. This discussion on godly rebellion will get your students thinking about how they want to live—in rebellion or conformity.

OPENER

Display this question to get students thinking about the topic at hand: HOW WOULD YOU DEFINE THE WORD REBEL? As you begin your time, have students come up with their own definitions. See how close their definitions come to one dictionary source (below). Have the following definition for rebel ready to unveil at the appropriate time (on a computer or video screen, a piece of paper, or a whiteboard). After comparing definitions, point them toward the TalkSheet.

> **Reb • el [n., adj. reb-uhl; v. ri-bel]**
> **noun, adjective, verb, -belled, -bel•ling.**
> **–noun**
> 1. a person who refuses allegiance to, resists, or rises in arms against the government or ruler of his or her country.
> 2. a person who resists any authority, control, or tradition.
>
> **–adjective**
> 3. rebellious; defiant.
> 4. of or pertaining to rebels.
>
> **–verb (used without object) rebel**
> 5. to reject, resist, or rise in arms against one's government or ruler.
> 6. to resist or rise against some authority, control, or tradition.
> 7. to show or feel utter repugnance: His very soul rebelled at spanking the child.

Dictionary.com Unabridged (v 1.1)
Based on the Random House Unabridged Dictionary,
© Random House, Inc. 2006.

THE DISCUSSION, BY NUMBERS

1. Make a list of all of your students' suggestions for rebels, real or fictional. These don't have to be people they know personally. Throw out a few suggestions to get them started. If you have Internet access in your meeting space, you might want to pull up pictures of some classic rebels, such as James Dean, Charles Manson, white supremacists, and rock stars with reputations of rebellion—just to get the creative juices flowing.
2. This question doesn't need a definitive answer. Lob it out there and see what you come up with.
3. Let them share stories of their friends' rebellion and the outcome. Be careful not to let the sharing get out of hand.
4. Now shift the focus from things their friends have done to the rebellious things your students have done. This is intended to be a time where they can laugh at their poor choices, rather than glorify them. Just remind them that wise people learn from their mistakes and fools repeat them.
5. Have them write Mark 10:45 on their sheets. Then have them discuss how Jesus' approach to life (serving others rather than being served, laying down his life as a ransom for many) could be viewed as one of rebellion. Challenge them to think about the stories they know about Jesus. Some examples might be when Jesus talked to the Samaritan woman at the well (John 4), the way Jesus consistently called out the religious leaders of the day, and how he chose to hang out with the "sinners."
6. Ask your group to consider the most "rebellious" things they could do in accordance with Jesus' way of life.
7. Discuss why more people, particularly your students' friends, don't choose to pattern their lives after the "rebellious" life of Jesus.
8. Have your group discuss the most difficult and challenging things about following Jesus' pattern for being a rebel.
9. What are the biggest benefits of choosing to be a "rebel" like Jesus? There doesn't have to be any right answer. Just let them consider the question and respond to it.

THE CLOSE

Ask them to consider one final question and email their answers to you sometime during the week. **If you chose to pattern your life after the "rebel" named Jesus, what would you like to be remembered for?** Close your time by praying over your group and the "rebellious" choices they might make in the week ahead.

MORE

• **Play the video of U2 performing "Sunday Bloody Sunday" from the *Live at Red Rocks* DVD as you start your session. Then have your group members discuss why U2's singer, Bono, says the song "is not a rebel song."**
• **Show your students the "Don't Tread on Me" flag of the American Revolution and share how it's a symbol that's been associated with not giving in to tyranny. Then, based on your discussion of Mark 10:45, have your students come up with their own "rebel flag" for your group. Provide the appropriate paints and materials for their creations.**
• **Ask your group to brainstorm some songs and come up with the ultimate playlist for a rebel.**

1. When you go to the food court at a mall, what free samples are being given away? What's your favorite?

2. Where else are you likely to be offered free samples?

3. What's the purpose of free samples?

4. Check out Luke 4:14-21. After reading this passage, how might Jesus be viewed as the One who offered free samples of what heaven and the kingdom of God are like?

5. Why might the following from the passage above be considered a good "free sample" of heaven and the kingdom of God?

- v. 18—good news proclaimed to the poor

- v. 18—freedom proclaimed for the prisoners

- v. 18—recovery of sight for the blind

- v. 18—set the oppressed free

- v. 19—proclaim the year of the Lord's favor

6. Check out Luke 4:31-37. What kind of free sample of heaven and the kingdom of God did Jesus allow people to taste in this passage?

7. Check out Luke 4:38-44. What kinds of free samples of heaven and the kingdom of God was Jesus passing out for people to try?

8. What kinds of free samples could you give out this week that would offer people a good taste of what Jesus and his kingdom are like—and make them want to come back for more?

THIS WEEK

What if Jesus' life and ministry were viewed as his offering free samples of heaven and the kingdom of God? This discussion will give your students a different perspective of how Jesus may have wanted to create an appetite for God through the life he demonstrated and offered to others.

OPENER

Start by showing your students a plate full of free samples that might be found at a food court in the mall, such as chicken nuggets, sandwich bites, small wedges of pizza, small spoons of ice cream, and samples of chocolate chip cookies. If you have enough samples for everyone, let your group have a taste while they answer question one on their TalkSheets.

THE DISCUSSION, BY NUMBERS

1. Have your group name the free samples that might be available if they were to go to the food court today. What are their favorites? Ask them to share the free samples they *wish* were offered.

2. You might want to get them started by suggesting a store like Bath and Body Works that might give out samples of lotion, or maybe a perfume or cologne sample in a department store. Consider mentioning that drug dealers will offer kids free samples to get them hooked.

3. Have your group brainstorm different purposes for providing free samples. Answers could include, "To get a taste of something to see if you like it," or "To try something you may not have tried," or "To help fill you up when you're hungry." Encourage them to think outside the box as they discuss their answers.

4. Now have your group read Luke 4:14-21 together, paying particular attention to verse 21 where Jesus says that everything he just read (originally from Isaiah 61:1-2) is fulfilled in him. These were all gestures that would have "tasted" good to his listeners.

5. Have your group spend some time talking about why the various elements from that passage might be viewed as a good "free sample."
   - v. 18—good news proclaimed to the poor *(The poor had nothing and were in need of hope.)*
   - v. 18—freedom proclaimed for the prisoners *(Freedom is what every prisoner longs for.)*
   - v. 18—recovery of sight to the blind *(A blind person longs to be able to see.)*
     - v. 18—set the oppressed free *(Oppressed people wish to be out from under the rule of the one who's controlling them.)*
     - v. 19—proclaim the year of the Lord's favor *(To this audience, who'd been longing for a Messiah, Jesus was speaking of the fulfillment of many years of anticipation and hardship.)*

   All of these elements would have been received with great joy had the religious leaders with their doubts and arguments not been present.

6. Continue developing the concept of Jesus handing out free samples of heaven and the kingdom of God by having your group look at Luke 4:31-37. In these verses Jesus gives out the free sample of his power, and the people are amazed at his authority over evil. If this is what heaven is like, then many were about to develop a taste for it.

7. In Luke 4:38-44 Jesus heals many people and continues his preaching ministry.

8. These may be challenging concepts for middle schoolers to grasp. Challenge them to put themselves in the place of the people mentioned in Luke 4. Why did they react that way? What kinds of free samples could they give to their friends and classmates that would say: "This is what Jesus, heaven, and the kingdom of God are like"?

THE CLOSE

Ask your group to consider the best sample of God they've ever received. Who gave it to them? What was it? How did they react when they received it? Challenge them to be intentional this week about giving away great free samples of God to others.

MORE

- **Take a field trip to the local food court and experience the free samples firsthand.**
- **Hand out small, plastic tasting spoons as a tangible reminder for your students to give their friends free samples of what heaven and the kingdom of God taste like.**
- **Make a list of creative ways your students could give free samples of heaven and the kingdom of God to the people around them.**

1. What do you think it means to have faith?

2. Describe some situations in which faith is required.

3. Name someone who lives a life of faith.

A PICTURE IS WORTH A THOUSAND WORDS

4. Check out the following stories in which Jesus mentions faith. In each story underline the word *faith*. Why did Jesus highlight the faith of these people?

- Mark 2:1-5

- Mark 4:35-41

- Mark 5:21-34

- Mark 6:1-6

- Mark 10:46-52

- Mark 11:22-25

- Mark 16:14

5. What's the biggest obstacle to having faith?

6. Describe a time in your life when you felt like you had great faith.

7. Describe a time in your life when you wish you'd had great faith.

8. Draw a picture of what your faith looks like at this time in your life.

32. A PICTURE IS WORTH A THOUSAND WORDS—Drawing a picture of faith

(Mark 2:1-5, 4:35-41, 5:21-34, 6:1-6, 10:46-52, 11:22-25, 16:14)

THIS WEEK

Faith is difficult to describe. It's been said that, "Faith isn't faith until it's all you're holding on to." Or, "You don't hold on to faith; faith holds on to you." This week's TalkSheet and discussion should help your students develop a better mental picture of what faith really is.

OPENER

Share with your group how some concepts may be difficult to get our minds around. Suggest to them that faith is one of those tricky concepts. Tell them you're going to have them answer a few questions about faith before asking them to participate in an exercise that will reveal their understanding of it.

THE DISCUSSION, BY NUMBERS

1. Ask your group to discuss what it means for a person to "have faith." After talking through some of their definitions, move on to the next question.
2. Let them share some situations in which they think faith would be required. If they're stumped, you might want to suggest something like walking across a wobbly bridge or sitting in a rocking chair. In both cases you have faith that the object will hold up under your weight.
3. Ask them to share some examples of people who live lives of faith. These can be both people they know and people they know of.
4. Let your group know that they're going to look at all the places in the Gospel of Mark where the topic of faith is mentioned. Have them divide up the passages listed and give their responses to the questions. Let them wrestle with why they believe Jesus chose to highlight the characteristic of faith. You don't always have to have an answer for your group. Sometimes the role of a teacher is simply to probe your students into thinking about things on a deeper level or from a different angle without giving them a "right" answer. See what they come up with on their own.
    - Mark 2:1-5 = Jesus forgives and heals a paralyzed man.
    - Mark 4:35-41 = Jesus calms the storm.
    - Mark 5:21-34 = Jesus heals a sick woman.
    - Mark 6:1-6 = Jesus doesn't do many miracles in Nazareth.
    - Mark 10:46-52 = Jesus heals a blind man.
    - Mark 11:22-25 = Jesus teaches about the power of faith in prayer.

- Mark 16:14 = Jesus appears to the Eleven and rebukes them.
5. Now ask them to talk through what they believe to be the biggest hindrances to faith. They'll likely respond with concepts such as fear or doubt. Ask them to share some examples to help them think about this question more concretely.
6. Have them consider questions six and seven together before answering them. After your group has had a moment to think about these, let them share both answers before moving on to question eight. To set the tone, you might want to go first and share about a time in your life when you felt as though you had great faith and a time when you *wish* you did.
7. See question six.
8. The concept of faith is a challenging one to define with words, so ask your students to consider it through art. Give them some art supplies and a few minutes to draw a picture of what their faith looks like at this time in their lives. Let them know they aren't expected to be perfect artists—just honest with themselves. Remind them of the saying, "A picture is worth a thousand words."

THE CLOSE

Ask your students to share their drawings with the group and explain what they represent. Encourage them to allow themselves the freedom to sketch and draw and utilize creative expressions as a tool when thinking about big ideas.

MORE

- **You could start by doing an object lesson about faith. Suggest that it takes faith to sit in a chair (as you demonstrate sitting down in a chair). At some point you have faith that the chair won't collapse.**
- **Ask your students to pair off and have one blindfold the other. The one without the blindfold should then lead her partner through a maze or obstacle course. The blindfolded students will have to exercise faith that their partners are leading them on the right path. After the first set of students have finished their faith walk, have the pairs switch places so everyone takes a turn being blindfolded.**
- **Play a song about faith such as Paul Baloche's "Open the Eyes of My Heart" or Rich Mullins' "Awesome God" and have a discussion with your group about the meaning behind the lyrics.**

1. What's your favorite game to play? What are the rules of that game?

2. What are the best and worst rules of that game?

3. Why are the rules necessary?

4. List the rules that you're supposed to follow in life.

5. What's the worst "life rule"?

6. Which rule is most helpful to you?

7. Check out Exodus 20:1-17. What are the 10 big rules that God gave us?

8. Why did God give us these 10 big rules?

9. What do God's rules in Exodus 20 say about what God values?

10. It's been said that rules without relationship equals rebellion. What do you think this means?

THIS WEEK

This TalkSheet focuses on the rules of our lives. With a little bit of discussion, your group may come to a new level of understanding about the Ten Commandments and how they help us not only be who God wants us to be but also learn more about what God values.

OPENER

Start by writing the name of a well-known game on a whiteboard or large piece of paper, such as BASKET-BALL, BASEBALL, CHECKERS, or MONOPOLY. Make sure your group knows how to play whichever game you choose. Have your students tell you all the rules of the game while you list them under the name of the game. Then have them answer questions one through three on their TalkSheets.

THE DISCUSSION, BY NUMBERS

1. Let your students share all three of their answers before moving on to question four.
2. Hopefully a theme will emerge as your group shares why they believe rules are necessary. Without rules, a person doesn't know how to play the game or how to win. The game would pretty much be an exercise in anarchy and frustration.
3. Encourage your students to explain the reasoning behind the two rules they chose—one they like, and one they dislike.
4. Make the point that there are a whole lot of rules in life. Have them make a list of all the "life rules" they can think of in a certain amount of time. Encourage them to think creatively and give them some examples of where to look, such as home, school, work, driving, and so on. After the time expires, have them share their lists.
5. Chances are good that your students don't care for a particular rule. Have them share the worst rule and why they dislike it so much.
6. Now have them share the most helpful rule and why they chose it.
7. At this point in the discussion, emphasize that God has some rules for our lives—The Ten Commandments. Have your group check out Exodus 20:1-17 and jot them down.
   - v. 3 = No other gods before God Almighty
   - v. 4 = No idols
   - v. 7 = No misusing the name of God
   - v. 8 = Remember the Sabbath day and keep it holy
   - v. 12 = Honor your dad and mom
   - v. 13 = Don't murder
   - v. 14 = Don't commit adultery
   - v. 15 = Don't steal
   - v. 16 = Don't give false testimony against your neighbor
   - v. 17 = Don't covet anything that belongs to your neighbor
8. Why did God choose these 10? Should a different rule have made the top 10?
9. What do the rules in Exodus 20 say about what God values? *(worship, life, community, peace, love, honesty, integrity, thankfulness, contentment, respect)*
10. Let them talk about their understanding of how rules, relationships, and rebellion go hand-in-hand if rules are instituted apart from a healthy relationship. People will usually respond better if they have a good relationship with the person who created the rules. Conversely, when the relationship is strained or nonexistent, rebellion is a more natural response.

THE CLOSE

Ask your group to consider the relationships they have with the people who've put rules over their lives. Have them talk through ways they might be able to make some progress in their relationships with their parents, teachers, coaches, and God. Close the session by praying for your students.

MORE

• **If you have time, expand question 10 and shift the focus to the rules their parents have made for their lives. What do those rules say about the things their parents value? Help them see things from a new perspective. It's fine to disagree with the rules in their lives. However, honoring mom and dad means respecting their rules.**
• **Talk through any situations or relationships in which they have the responsibility or authority to make or set rules over someone else. How does that responsibility make them feel? What's it like when someone disobeys or breaks one of the rules they've set up?**
• **Challenge your group to make up a new game and then play it. Afterward, discuss what they learned from the experience. Would they change the rules? Did they like what they came up with? What was the hardest thing about creating the new game? What was the easiest thing about it?**

1. If your house was on fire and you had time to take only one possession with you, what would it be?

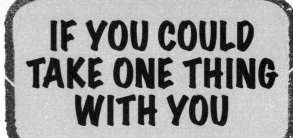

IF YOU COULD TAKE ONE THING WITH YOU

2. If you could grab one thing for each member of your family, what would you take?

3. What would be the hardest thing for you to leave behind?

4. Check out Luke 23:32-43. What did Jesus choose to take with him to paradise (v. 43)?

5. Based on your answer to question four, what does Jesus value?

6. What things make it easy to value other people?

7. What things make it hard to value other people?

8. What's one thing you can do this week to show others that you value them?

THIS WEEK

This discussion centers on how much Jesus values people. When Jesus chose to take one thing with him from death into paradise, he chose a person—the thief hanging on the cross next to him. If Jesus values people this much, perhaps we should do the same.

OPENER

Start by showing your most prized possession. It doesn't have to be worth a lot of money. It could be something with lots of sentimental value. Talk about why it's valuable and then have your students name some things that are valuable to them. After giving your group a few minutes to share, have them read question one on their TalkSheets to continue the discussion.

THE DISCUSSION, BY NUMBERS

1. Make sure your students realize that their family and pets would already be out of the house in this scenario. Ask them to explain why that particular item holds so much value for them.
2. Now have your group share about the items they'd take if they could go back and get something for each of their family members. What do their family members value the most?
3. Let your group share about the hardest thing they'd have to leave behind. Why would it be so hard to leave it?
4. Ask someone to read Luke 23:32-43. Then ask your group what Jesus chose to take with him to paradise (v. 43). *(Answer: The thief on the cross next to him.)*
5. Have them share their thoughts about what Jesus values the most, based on this passage. Basically, Jesus values people so much that as he's dying on the cross, he decided to take this man to be with him in paradise after they died.
6. Take a few minutes and have your group discuss the things that make it easy for them to value other people. You may want to offer a few examples, such as a good personality, a good sense of humor, great athletic ability, a pretty face, generosity, and so on.
7. Now have your group consider what makes it challenging to value other people, such as an ungrateful attitude, arrogance, a gossip, or being judgmental.
8. Wrap up the discussion by asking each person in your group to come up with one creative way to show that they value other people. Then challenge them to do it throughout the week.

THE CLOSE

Give each person a small piece of paper with the question, "What do I value?" written on it as a reminder of the discussion. Ask them to pray with the paper in their hands this week and encourage them to ask God to give them a heart that truly values other people like Jesus does.

MORE
• Before your students talk about the things they value most, play the scene from *The Sound of Music* in which Julie Andrews sings "My Favorite Things."
• Have the discussion about questions one through three around a campfire.
• Invite someone who's experienced losing their home in a fire to share their experience with your group.

1. If you could trade places with anybody on the planet, who would it be and why?

IS LIFE WORKING FOR YOU?

2. List some signs that show a person's life is working.

3. What are some signs that a person's life isn't working?

4. What's one thing you keep doing that isn't working for you and wish were different?

5. Check out Proverbs 26:11. What does it mean?

6. Insanity has been defined as "Doing the same things over and over again and expecting different results." What do you think this definition has to do with Proverbs 26:11?

7. What do you think the definition for *insanity* and Proverbs 26:11 have to do with your answer to question four?

8. In the areas of your life that aren't working, what do you need to do differently?

THIS WEEK

When it comes to the areas of our lives that aren't working, we must choose to make some changes or life still won't work. To think otherwise is a good definition of insanity: "Doing the same thing over and over again and expecting different results."

OPENER

Start by describing someone with whom you'd love to trade places for a while because of how life seems to be working for that person. Set the parameters for the hypothetical any way you want to do it. You could trade places for a day, a week, a month, a year, or even a lifetime. Describe what it is about the person's life that makes you want to trade places. The object is to lead your group into thinking about the same scenario based on things that you—and in a moment, they—assume are working well in the other person's life. Maybe the person you'd like to trade places with has a lot of money, freedom, skills, fame, opportunities, or physical attributes that you desire. After you've opened the session with your answer, have your group answer the same question on their TalkSheets.

DISCUSSION

1. Ask your group to write the name of someone they'd trade places with and what it is about that person's life that makes them want to do so. Let your group share their answers before moving on to the next question.
2. Tell your group that the reason they picked that person in the first question is because something (or things) in that person's life is "working." Have your group list the top signs that a person's life is working. You may want to offer a few examples, such as popularity, good health, good looks, wealth, and so on.
3. Flip the question and ask your group to list the signs that a person's life is not working. Some examples might be acne, being out of shape, not having many friends, and so on.
4. The idea is to talk about bad habits that are causing them to be someone they don't want to be. You may need to set the tone for this question by being vulnerable (yet appropriate!) and sharing

something out of your own life that's become a pattern or habit that isn't working for you.
5. Have your group turn to Proverbs 26:11 and read it out loud. After they've written what the verse means in their own words, let your group share their thoughts before you share yours. You may want to tell them something like: **If you keep doing the same things, you'll keep getting the same results. Unless you choose to take a different approach, you'd be foolish to believe you'll ever have a different outcome from going back to the same poor choice or bad habit over and over again.**
6. Read the definition of *insanity* to your group and ask them to make the connection between the definition and what God says to us in Proverbs 26:11. Ask what the two have in common.
7. Now have your group think about what they just answered on question six and then relate that answer to whatever bad habit they wrote down for question four.
8. Ask your students to share one thing they'll try to do differently this week.

THE CLOSE

Offer your group a bit of vision: Challenge them to think about what their lives would look like if each month they committed to changing one thing that isn't working for them and then did this for 12 months. Challenge them to write down one area they'll commit to start working on this week.

MORE

• **For the coming week, challenge your group to write a list of all the things that are working for them and a list of things that aren't working. They should then select three things from the "not working" list to focus on changing throughout the coming year.**

• **Bring a dog to the meeting to help make the point in Proverbs 26:11. The dog doesn't have to vomit. However, sometimes just having a prop to make the verse come alive will make it more memorable.**

• **Have your students send you an email about what they'd like for their lives to look like if they had the strength and courage to "be different" than they are now. What would be the first thing they'd change to make their lives begin working for them?**

1. What do you like about family vacations?

2. What do you dislike about family vacations?

3. What do you like about coming home after being away?

4. Who said Jesus would come back after being away?

   • Matthew 24:42-44; John 14:1-3; Revelation 22:12

   • Acts 1:10-11

   • 1 Thessalonians 4:16

   • Hebrews 9:28

   • 2 Peter 3:10

   • 1 John 3:2; Revelation 1:7; Revelation 22:12, 20

5. What does the Bible say we should do until Jesus does come back?

   • Matthew 24:42-44

   • Titus 2:12-13

   • James 5:8

6. When does the Bible say Jesus will come back?

   • Matthew 24:42-44

   • Matthew 25:13

   • Mark 13:32-37

   • Luke 12:40

   • 1 Thessalonians 5:1-11

7. How should a person "get ready" for Jesus' return?

36. SEE YOU REAL SOON—Exploring when Jesus will come back *(Matthew 24:42-44, 25:13; Mark 13:32-37; Luke 12:40; John 14:1-3; Acts 1:10-11; 1 Thessalonians 4:16, 5:1-11; Titus 2:12-13; Hebrews 9:28; James 5:8; 2 Peter 3:10; 1 John 3:2; Revelation 1:7, 22:12, 20)*

THIS WEEK

This TalkSheet reveals what the Bible says about Jesus' return to earth. Your students will discuss what Jesus and others in the New Testament said about him coming back and what people should do in the meantime.

OPENER

Divide your group into teams and start with a competition to see how many Disney shows they can name in five minutes. After the allotted time is up, see who has the most shows listed and give the winning team a prize. If nobody has *The Mickey Mouse Club* on their lists, make sure you mention it. Then share how this show aired on TV from 1955 to 1959, and at the end of every show, the Mouseketeers would sing this song:

> Now it's time to say good-bye to all our company.
> M-I-C
> See you real soon.
> K-E-Y
> Why? Because we like you!
> M-O-U-S-E.

Now turn the group's attention to the TalkSheet questions.

THE DISCUSSION, BY NUMBERS

1. Chances are good they've been on at least one family vacation. Ask them to share what they liked most about it.
2. Now flip the question and have them talk about what they don't like about family vacations. You may want to share some of your own likes and dislikes to get the conversation started.
3. Ask your group to share what they like the most about returning home after a trip. You may have to offer some examples, such as getting some time away from the family, seeing their friends, sleeping in their own bed.
4. The Bible teaches that Jesus has said he will come back to this place one day. Take some time to read the words of some people who spoke about Jesus coming back to earth. Have your group write the name of the person who said it next to each Scripture reference.
   - Matthew 24:44; John 14:1-3; Revelation 22:12 (Jesus)
   - Acts 1:10-11 (two angels)
   - 1 Thessalonians 4:16 (Paul)
   - Hebrews 9:28 (the author of Hebrews—scholars aren't certain who it is)
   - 2 Peter 3:10 (Peter)
   - 1 John 3:2; Revelation 1:7; Revelation 22:12, 20 (John)

5. Now have your group look up some passages that talk about what we should do before Jesus comes back. Have them write their answers and then share them with the group.
   - Matthew 24:42-44 (keep watch and be ready)
   - Titus 2:12-13 (say no to ungodliness and worldly passions; live self-controlled, upright, and godly lives)
   - James 5:8 (be patient and stand firm)
6. Now ask your group to look at some passages that speak about the time when Jesus will return. Have them write their answers and share them with the group.
   - Matthew 24:42-44 (at an hour when you don't expect him)
   - Matthew 25:13 (you don't know the day or the hour)
   - Mark 13:32-37 (no one knows the day or hour)
   - Luke 12:40 (at an hour when you don't expect him)
   - 1 Thessalonians 5:1-11 (like a thief in the night, v. 2)
7. Wrap up the discussion by asking your group how a person should get ready for Jesus' return. They may talk about making changes in their lives, making amends with people, as well as making decisions. Affirm these things and then be sure to talk with them about what the Bible says concerning salvation. Many of the above passages link Jesus' return with salvation from sin and death.

THE CLOSE

Ask your students what they need to do today in order to "be ready" for when Jesus comes back. Pray for them before they leave.

MORE

- **Arrange to show part of an episode of the original *The Mickey Mouse Club*—at least the end of the show when they sing the closing song. (Episodes can be found on a series of DVDs called Walt Disney Treasures: The Mickey Mouse Club; they're available for purchase online.)**
- **For more interaction on the discussion about family vacations, provide a map of either the world or the United States and a box of pushpins—then let your group pin all of the places where they've vacationed with their family and friends.**
- **If it's appropriate in the context of your group setting, you may want to give your group an opportunity to trust Jesus as their Savior. Extend the invitation to your group or arrange for one of the other leaders or pastors to talk with your group about this decision in more detail.**

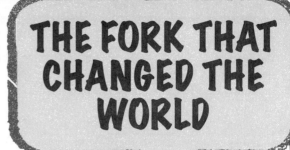
THE FORK THAT CHANGED THE WORLD

1. Someone once said, "Your next action could change the world, so make it a good one." List four actions (from throughout the course of history) that various people made when they came to a "fork in the road" and changed the world for the better.

2. Now list four actions that changed the world for the worse.

3. Describe one of your actions that changed your life for the worse.

4. Describe one of your actions that changed your life for the better.

5. Which of your actions has changed the world the most? Was it for the better or for the worse?

6. Check out Galatians 6:7-8. What do you think these verses have to do with the quote from question one?

7. List four actions that were taken by various people in the Bible that changed the world for the better.

8. What's the most world-changing action you could take this week?

37. THE FORK THAT CHANGED THE WORLD—Every decision we make could change the world for better or for worse (Galatians 6:7-8)

THIS WEEK
This TalkSheet will help your students understand that every decision has ramifications that can change the world for good or for bad. Your students must be consistently mindful of the choices they make—all day, every day.

OPENER
Begin your time together by asking your group to consider the metaphor "a fork in the road." Have them discuss the meaning and then let them know that this saying refers to when someone faces one or more options as they travel down the road of life. Ask your group to share examples of when they found themselves at a "fork in the road" and what they did as a result. After each person has had an opportunity to share, have your students consider the quote in question one on the TalkSheet.

THE DISCUSSION, BY NUMBERS

1. Ask your group to consider the quote: "Your next action could change the world, so make it a good one." Let them discuss what this means as it corresponds to the "fork in the road" metaphor. Then have your group list four actions that changed the world for the better. Have them name people who aren't in the Bible because the discussion will head that way later on.

2. Flip the question and have students list four actions that changed the world for the worse. Then have your group discuss their answers.

3. Now make the discussion more personal. Have them consider one action that changed their own lives for the worse.

4. After they've discussed their negative actions, have your group consider one action that changed their lives for the better.

5. Now ask your group to consider the other people their actions have impacted. What action has had the most affect on the world—good or bad? Why did they mention that particular action?

6. Ask someone to read aloud Galatians 6:7-8. Then ask your group about the correlation between these verses and the quote in question one. The passage speaks of people reaping what they sow in life. If people make poor decisions based on their sinful desires, then destruction will result.

Conversely, if people make wise decisions, then they'll yield good fruit that blesses many.

7. Ask your group to list the actions of four people in the Bible who changed the world for the better. Depending on their level of biblical understanding, you may need to prime the pump a bit. Some obvious answers could be Jesus' death, burial, and resurrection, which certainly changed the world for the better. The disciples' choice to follow Jesus changed the world for the better. Noah's choice to build the ark saved his family and the animals from extinction. These are just a few examples that might help your group answer this question.

8. Now bring the discussion back to where your group lives: Ask them to consider one action they could take this week that would most likely change their world for the better. Ask them to be realistic but to think about an action they could take that would have ramifications on a larger scale. Let your group share their answers before wrapping up the discussion with The Close.

THE CLOSE
Challenge your students this week to remember the discussion each time they pick up a fork to eat their meals. Close your group time by praying for your students.

MORE
• Make Sharpie markers available to your group and have them write GALATIANS 6:7-8 on plastic forks as a reminder that the decisions they make will have consequences for the good or for the bad. Challenge them to read these verses every day as a way to remember what your group talked about during this discussion.
• Every day this week, text or email your students the following question: WHAT ACTION DID YOU TAKE TODAY THAT COULD HAVE CHANGED THE WORLD? Tell your students you'll do this throughout the week as a way to help them think about the decisions they make when they come to their own forks in the road each day.
• Watch the movie *Pay It Forward* as a group. Ask your students to consider how the characters' actions throughout the movie changed the world for the better. As with any film, be sure to preview it to make sure the content is suitable for your group. You may also want to request permission from your students' parents beforehand.

1. The weirdest thing I've ever done in my life is…

2. The weirdest thing I've ever eaten is…

3. The weirdest movie I've ever seen is…

4. The weirdest place I've ever been is…

5. The weirdest thing about my parents is…

6. Check out the following passages and list the weird stuff that three Old Testament prophets did to help communicate God's message to people.

- Isaiah 20

- Jeremiah 27

- Ezekiel 4

7. It's been said that "sometimes you have to look beyond the weirdness to understand what something means." What's the meaning behind each of these Old Testament prophets' weird actions?

- Isaiah

- Jeremiah

- Ezekiel

8. Check out Isaiah 55:8-9 and write what you think these verses have to do with looking beyond the weirdness to understand what something means.

BEYOND THE WEIRDNESS

THIS WEEK

This TalkSheet will show your group some of the weird things that Old Testament prophets did in order to communicate God's message to his people. In such moments, we must choose to obey and look beyond the weirdness in order to understand what something means.

OPENER

Begin by showing your students some pictures from *www.weirdomatic.com* to get your group thinking about all things weird. Be aware that some material may not be suitable for all groups; use your best judgment when choosing what to show them. After you have their attention, have your group share a few thoughts on weird things by pointing them toward the TalkSheet questions.

THE DISCUSSION, BY NUMBERS

1. Have your group take a few moments to complete the sentences in questions one through five. Then go around the group and have each person share an answer for question one, then for question two, and so on.
2. See question one.
3. See question one.
4. See question one.
5. See question one.
6. Tell your group that the Old Testament is filled with some stuff that seems pretty weird at first glance. Then have them look up the passages about three Old Testament prophets and write down the weird stuff that Isaiah, Jeremiah, and Ezekiel did to communicate God's message in an unforgettable manner.
   - Isaiah walked around naked for three years among the people of Jerusalem.
   - Jeremiah walked the streets with a wooden yoke around his neck.
   - Ezekiel carved a model of Jerusalem into a brick. He lied beside the model on his left side for 390 days. Then he turned to his right side and lied beside it for another 40 days. During these 430 days, he was to eat only bread cooked over burning cow dung.
7. Have your group consider this quote: "Sometimes you have to look beyond the weirdness to understand what something means." Then see if your group can come up with the following meanings behind the weird actions of these three prophets.
   - Isaiah: It was symbolism regarding what would happen if Judah aligned itself with Egypt and Ethiopia: They'd be conquered, and everyone would end up naked captives.
   - Jeremiah: The yoke symbolized the yoke of Babylonian rule.
   - Ezekiel: This 430-day exhibition symbolized the years that Israel and Judah would be in exile after the Babylonians conquered them and what their lives would be like.
8. Ask someone to read aloud Isaiah 55:8-9. Then ask your group to talk through what they think those verses have to do with looking beyond the weirdness to understand the meaning of something. Sometimes what may seem weird to us is simply an indication that we don't have the same perspective that God does. This is where trust and faithful obedience to God come into play. Perhaps we'll one day know the meaning behind the weirdness. But as followers of Jesus, our best option is to trust and obey what God tells us to do—no matter how weird it seems—as long as it doesn't contradict what the Bible says.

THE CLOSE

Of all the stuff that Jesus tells his followers to do, what do you think is the weirdest thing he might be telling you to do this week? Have your group share their answers and then close your time by praying that whatever weird things Jesus may lead them to do throughout their lives, may God give them boldness to live the weirdness and seek the meaning behind it along the way.

MORE

- **Check out www.weirdal.com for some hilarious parodies of music videos by Weird Al Yankovic.**
- **The city motto for Austin, Texas, is "Keep Austin Weird." For other weird ideas that might be helpful to your discussion, check out *www.keepaustinweird. com* for all kinds of links. (Some are more appropriate than others.) One thing that's popular in Austin is "Keep Austin Weird" merchandise. Have your group make their own "weird" T-shirts. Whatever the name of your group, team, or ministry might be, just insert it between the words *Keep* and *Weird* and start a new trend with your group.**

1. When it comes to middle school: I assume that…

2. When it comes to my friends: I assume that…

3. When it comes to my family: I assume that…

4. When it comes to food: I assume that…

5. When it comes to my health: I assume that…

6. When it comes to my schoolwork: I assume that…

7. When it comes to curfew: I assume that…

8. When it comes to music: I assume that…

9. When it comes to money: I assume that…

10. When it comes to television: I assume that…

11. When it comes to the computer: I assume that…

12. When it comes to Jesus: I assume that…

13. In Matthew 6:1-18 Jesus assumes at least three things about his followers. What does the Bible say Jesus assumes in the following verses:

   • Matthew 6:1-4

   • Matthew 6:5-15

   • Matthew 6:16-18

THIS WEEK

This TalkSheet will lead your group to explore a few assumptions that Jesus has about all people who claim to be his followers. If his assumptions and our realities don't match up, what needs to happen in order for our lives to get in sync with Jesus' assumptions?

OPENER

Ask your group what it means to assume something. You want to get your students on the same page regarding the definition of this word or concept. So "to assume something" as it pertains to this discussion will mean, "to take for granted that something can be counted upon to happen or to be true." Have your group take a few minutes to fill in their answers on questions one through 12 before talking about the things they assume.

THE DISCUSSION, BY NUMBERS

1. Have your group answer questions one through 12 on their own. Then go back and let each of your students share what they wrote for each question. Let the whole group share their answers to question one, then question two, and so forth.
2. See question one.
3. See question one.
4. See question one.
5. See question one.
6. See question one.
7. See question one.
8. See question one.
9. See question one.
10. See question one.
11. See question one.
12. See question one.
13. Now make the point that we have assumptions about all kinds of things in our lives. Then let them know that Jesus also has assumptions about the way we live. Jesus spells out at least three assumptions for those who claim to be his followers in Matthew 6:1-18. Have them turn to this passage and then write down and discuss Jesus' assumptions from each of the following sections.
    - Matthew 6:1-4. Read this section and then have them write down Jesus' assumption from verse 2 *(when you give to the needy)*. Not if you give but *when* you give. Then ask them how they're doing in this area.
    - Matthew 6:5-15. Read this section and then have them write down Jesus' assumption in verse 5 *(when you pray)*. Not if you pray, *when* you pray. Then ask them how they're doing in this area: What do they pray for? How often do they pray? When do they pray? What response have they received from God? Point out that prayer isn't supposed to be just a listing of our wants and needs. It should be a two-way conversation.
    - Matthew 6:16-18. Read this section and then have them write down Jesus' assumption in verse 16 *(when you fast)*. Not if you fast, *when* you fast. Then ask them how they're doing in this area: How do they fast (do they give up food, music, the TV, the computer)? What's the hardest thing about it? Why do it?

THE CLOSE

Have your group write down this quote about these three assumptions from Matthew 6.

> When you give, it reminds you that there is somebody worse off than you. When you pray, it reminds you that someone is listening to you. When you fast, it reminds you that someone is sustaining you.—Neil McClendon

Ask your group to talk about what this quote means. Do they agree or disagree? Are Jesus' assumptions being lived out in the lives of your students who claim to be his followers? If not, do Jesus' assumptions need to change, or do we need to do some things differently—things that he assumes we're already doing? Have your group write down one thing they'll begin doing this week to make Jesus' assumption a reality in their lives.

MORE

- **Take a video camera and do a simple "man on the street" interview with various people. Have them answer this one question: "What do you assume?" See what answers you get and show the video at the beginning of the session to create some interest in this topic.**
- **Determine a specific time and way that your group will individually give, pray, and fast this week.**

1. Name something that God has made you good at doing.

SET APART

2. What do you wish God had made you good at doing that you just aren't?

3. Check out what Psalm 4:3 has to say about setting people apart. Write out the verse below.

4. What do you think it means to be faithful?

5. What do you think it means to be "set apart"?

6. If God were to set you apart for one thing on earth, what would that be?

7. Why does God set apart for himself those who are faithful?

8. In what area of your life would you consider yourself to be faithful?

9. In what area of your life do you need to do some work before you could be considered a faithful person?

THIS WEEK

This TalkSheet will offer your students a look at what it means to live faithfully and set apart for God in the things God designed them to do. Living faithfully in the life God has given us brings great pleasure to God and satisfaction to us as God's creation.

OPENER

Start by talking about Eric Liddell, a Scotsman whose story was portrayed in the 1981 Academy Award-winning film *Chariots of Fire*. Mention how Eric was a Christian who was trying to discern God's plan for his life regarding doing mission work in China or training to run in the 1924 Olympics for Scotland. Show the clip from *Chariots of Fire* in which Eric (played by Ian Charleson) says, "I believe that God made me for a purpose, for China. But he also made me fast. And when I run, I feel His pleasure." God made Eric Liddell good at running fast. And when he ran fast, he was fulfilling part of God's purpose for his life, thus allowing him to enjoy his life and bring pleasure to God at the same time. After your group has considered how Eric was created by God to run fast, have them consider question one on their TalkSheets to begin the discussion.

THE DISCUSSION, BY NUMBERS

1. Have your group members write down at least one thing God has made them good at doing. Then have your group share their answers with each other.

2. Now have them write down at least one thing they *wish* God had made them good at. Maybe it's something they enjoy doing but aren't very talented in that area. Maybe it's something they wish they liked to do, but they don't.

3. Have your group write out Psalm 4:3.

4. The students should answer questions four and five before sharing their responses with the group. Whatever they come up with is fine. The point is to get them thinking about the text and what God is saying through the verse. Resist the urge to give them "the answer."

5. Again, it's more important that they learn how to think critically about what God is saying through the Bible and how it might apply to their lives.

6. Remind them that God made Eric Liddell set apart to become a great runner. Eric knew this, and he fulfilled his purpose in life by doing what God created him to do. If God desires all of his creations to live this way, what do your students think God has created them to be set apart for?

7. Point them back to the Eric Liddell quote (from Opener). God sets apart those who are faithful because they bring God pleasure in the way they live their lives. Help them connect the dots before moving on: God needs nothing. However, God gets great pleasure from his creation. Thus, the creation that brings God pleasure is likely to get set apart for God's continued enjoyment.

8. Have your group talk about areas of their lives in which they'd consider themselves faithful.

9. Have them name at least one area in which they need to do some work before they can consider themselves faithful.

THE CLOSE

Wrap up the conversation by giving each student an index card with PSALM 4:3 and the verse printed on it. Encourage them to take the cards and commit the verse to memory this week. Close in prayer. Then each day of the coming week, text the word FAITHFUL to your students as a reminder of your discussion about faithfulness and how God wants us to live as one who is set apart.

MORE

• **Share with your students the context of Psalm 4. The author, King David, had been accused of something he didn't do. This Psalm is David's prayer, and he asks God to remember his innocence by the way he's lived his life in faithful obedience. In a sense, it's through the prayer that David remembers the good choices he'd made to live faithfully, thus causing him to realize that God knew he was innocent.**

• **Watch the entire *Chariots of Fire* film with your group. Serve some popcorn and drinks and just hang out together before discussing the TalkSheet.**

• **Lots of goofy videos have been made using "*Vangelis*," the theme song from Chariots of Fire, as the soundtrack. Have your group make its own video set to this infamous slow-motion music and see who creates the funniest one.**

1. What rules do your friends or family live by when it comes to saving seats?

2. Describe a situation when you tried to find a seat and there were none available.

3. What does it feel like when someone tells you the seat is saved?

4. Describe a time when you've been asked to save seats for others.

5. Describe a time when you had the best seat at an event.

6. Check out Luke 14:7-11. What did Jesus have to say about seating arrangements? How might these verses apply to your life?

7. Describe a time when you felt like the person who was asked to move so someone else could sit where you were sitting.

8. Describe a time in your life when someone was asked to move so you could have their seat.

9. When it comes to the way you approach sitting with your friends, which word best describes the way you try to find a place to sit—*exalted* or *humble*. Why?

THIS WEEK

This TalkSheet examines what Jesus had to say about being mindful of others. In middle school culture, *where* someone sits says a lot about who's exalted and who's humbled. Choosing not to save seats while being intentional about including everyone could be a great step toward becoming more like Jesus.

OPENER

Start with a game of musical chairs. Begin with one less chair than you have players and circle the chairs. Have students walk around the circle until the music stops, and then have everyone quickly find a chair to sit in. The person left standing is out of the game. Remove one chair and repeat the process until only one chair and two people remain. Whoever is seated at the end of the game is the winner. Talk about how finding a seat, and more importantly the "right" seat, is a huge deal to most people—especially in middle school. Then ask the students to take a look at their TalkSheets.

THE DISCUSSION, BY NUMBERS

1. People have different rules when it comes to saving seats. Maybe a code word like "shotgun" must be said before sitting in the front seat of a car. Perhaps there's an unspoken rule about a seat being saved when a person leaves to get something. Have some fun with this and let your group talk through their rules for saving seats.
2. Have your group talk about a time when they couldn't find a place to sit at a ballgame, movie, or even the lunch table.
3. Ask students to talk about how they felt—or think they'd feel—if they tried to sit somewhere and were told the seat was saved.
4. The group should now describe a time when they were asked to save seats for someone. How did they feel when they turned people away? How did people respond?
5. Have your group share about a time when they had the best seat in the house at a game or event. What made it so great? What did they have to do to get those seats?
6. Ask someone to read Luke 14:7-11 out loud, then discuss what Jesus said about seating arrangements. Basically, Jesus applauds those who choose to take the worst seats because they do so from a mindset of humility, as opposed to those who exalt themselves by taking the best seats. Ask how this passage might apply to your students' lives. Challenge them to think about seats in the lunchroom or on a bus.
7. Have your group discuss how they felt when they were asked to move so someone else could have their seat.
8. Now flip the scenario. Have them describe a time when someone was asked to move so they could be seated. What was the situation and how did they feel in that moment?
9. In Luke 14:7-11, Jesus says there are two approaches we can take: Exaltation or humility. Ask your group which word most accurately describes their current approach and why.

THE CLOSE

Challenge your group not to save seats when they gather with friends this week. Remind them that not having a place to sit can make someone feel excluded. Encourage them to be on the lookout for students who could use a seat at their table. Such an act of humility and selflessness will bring a smile to Jesus' face.

MORE

• **Watch two clips from *Forrest Gump*. The first is when young Forrest (played by Michael Conner Humphreys) gets on the school bus and tries to find a seat, only to hear "Seat's taken" over and over again. When he finally gets to where Jenny (played by Hanna Hall) is sitting, she says, "You can sit here." Later in the film, a grown-up Forrest (played by Tom Hanks) boards a bus bound for basic training, only to find things haven't changed much since childhood. When Bubba (played by Mykelti Williamson) lets Forrest sit next to him, they become fast friends, just as Forrest and Jenny did so many years earlier.**
• **Challenge your group to intentionally sit by someone they don't normally sit with at lunch. Encourage them to include people who don't normally sit with them and their friends or those who typically sit alone.**
• **In the coming week, challenge your group to call for "the worst" seat when they're going somewhere. Instead of calling "shotgun" to ride in the front seat, have them call "back-middle" as an intentional reminder of today's conversation and the things Jesus talked about in Luke 14:7-11.**

1. Who's like a guardian angel to you?

2. What are the characteristics of a guardian angel?

EVERY TIME A BELL RINGS

3. Check out James 5:16 and write the verse below.

4. What comes to mind when you read the following words in that verse?

   • Righteous

   • Powerful

   • Effective

5. Why do you pray?

6. Where do you pray?

7. How do you pray?

8. When do you pray?

9. In the film clip, Zuzu said, "Every time a bell rings, an angel gets his wings." How many bells are there during your normal school day?

10. What might happen if you committed to pray every time you heard a bell ring?

THIS WEEK

This TalkSheet focuses your group with a strategy to intentionally pray about something or someone. Utilize the school day and let the bells that signal the start and end of each class serve as a call to intentional, focused, and scheduled prayer for your group throughout the week.

OPENER

Ask your group to name some of their favorite Christmas movies. Make a master list and ask volunteers to share one of their favorite scenes. After everyone has had a chance to share, take a minute to set up the background for the 1946 classic *It's a Wonderful Life*. Show the last scene in the movie where the bell on the Christmas tree rings and Zuzu (played by Karolyn Grimes) says: "Look, Daddy. Teacher says, every time a bell rings an angel gets his wings." After the clip finishes, explain that George Bailey (played by Jimmy Stewart) had a guardian angel named Clarence, and Clarence just received his "wings" for helping George see the value of his life.

THE DISCUSSION, BY NUMBERS

1. Clarence, one of the main characters in *It's a Wonderful Life*, is George Bailey's guardian angel. Ask your group to think about who might be like a "guardian angel" for them. Are they like a guardian angel to anyone? A younger sibling? A neighbor?
2. Have your group list the qualities and characteristics of a "guardian angel."
3. James 5:16 says, "Therefore confess your sins to each other and pray for each other so that you may be healed. The prayer of a righteous person is powerful and effective."
4. Have your group discuss their definitions of the following words from James 5:16—righteous, powerful, and effective. What do these words mean? How can a person become someone who's described this way?
5. Give your group a few minutes and ask them to answer questions five through eight now. Then unpack these four questions one at a time with the group.

6. See question five.
7. See question five.
8. See question five.
9. Your students should count the number of bells they hear during a typical school day—first bell, tardy bells, the lunch bell, and so on—and write that number down.
10. Now ask your group to consider what might happen if they all committed to pray every time they hear a bell ring this week. How would it change them as individuals?

THE CLOSE

Ask your students to each think of someone who needs prayer. Encourage your group to take the "Every Time a Bell Rings" prayer challenge this week. Ask them to share about their experiences when you gather next week.

MORE

• During the Christmas season, gather to watch *It's a Wonderful Life* together. Afterward, work through the TalkSheet with your group.
• Give each person a small bell, such as a jingle bell, as a reminder to pray intentionally about something or someone.
• Suggest that your students take the time to write down one of their prayers each day. As they write, they could include things they've observed and learned during this time of intentional prayer.

1. Who's the strongest person you know?

2. What makes a person strong?

3. One definition for the word *weight* is "importance or influence." List five things that have good
   "weight" with you.

WEIGHT PROBLEM

4. Check out Exodus 20:12 and write the verse in the space below.

5. What do you think it means to honor your father and mother?

6. Why do you think God decided to give so much "weight" or importance to that command?

7. Check out the following verses and write in one sentence what you hear God saying to you about your
   relationship with your parents: Luke 2:51, Ephesians 6:1-3, and Colossians 3:20.

8. List some recent examples of things your parents told you that you've given weight to.

9. List some recent examples of things your parents told you that you haven't given weight to.

THIS WEEK

This TalkSheet will allow your students to take a closer look at what it means to "honor" their parents. After learning the significance God puts on the fifth commandment, your students will understand just how weighty this parent-child relationship issue is.

OPENER

Start off with a weight-lifting contest to see who can hold a certain amount of weight the longest. Although, the heavier the weight, the quicker the contest will end. The contestants should hold the weight(s) in their hands. When you say, "Go!" they'll stretch out their arms in front of them (parallel to the floor) or straight over their heads. The last one left holding up the weight is the winner. After the contest, have your group begin answering the questions on their TalkSheets.

THE DISCUSSION, BY NUMBERS

1. Get your group talking by asking them to name the strongest person they know.
2. Now have your group talk through what it means for a person to be "strong."
3. Point out the definition of the word *weight* on their TalkSheets. Explain that when someone influences you, it's said that person "carries a lot of weight" with you. Based on this definition, have your group share five things that carry weight with them.
4. Tell your group that God spells out some pretty weighty commands in Exodus 20—the Ten Commandments. Tell them to look up Exodus 20:12 and copy down the fifth commandment: "Honor your father and your mother…"
5. Have your group write and discuss what it means to "honor" their parents. Refrain from offering your thoughts until after they've finished talking through questions five and six.
6. Now have them talk about why God gave so much "weight" or importance to this command. Then take the opportunity to do a bit of teaching before moving on to the next question. Let them know that the Hebrew word for honor (*kabod*, pronounced "kuh-vode") is defined as "give weight to." God is literally saying, "Give weight to your parents." The first relationship most people have is with their parents. Therefore, if our relationship with our folks isn't right, then we'll probably struggle in our other relationships, too. As challenging as that concept might be, this is God's ideal when it comes to how we relate to other people.

7. Have your group look up Luke 2:51, Ephesians 6:1-3, and Colossians 3:20, and write one sentence about what God is saying to them about their relationship with their parents.
8. Ask your students to consider what their parents have said to them recently. What things have they given weight to (treated as important)? Let them write their answer for question eight and then move on to question nine before sharing both answers with the group.
9. Have your group consider the things their parents have said to them that they haven't given much weight to. Ask them to write these things and then share their answers for questions eight and nine.

Note: Some parent-child relationships are strained due to divorce, abandonment, or other difficulties. And when parents aren't involved in their children's lives, their words and actions won't carry as much weight. However, God still calls children to honor their parents. Before children can truly honor their parents, perhaps they must forgive them. Be sensitive to this issue—there are no easy answers. Be a good listener and encourage your students to continue processing how God wants them to honor Mom and Dad in the midst of their circumstances.

THE CLOSE

Before they go, ask your students to share one thing they'll do to honor their fathers and mothers this week. Then challenge them to pray for their relationship with their parents before you pray for all of your students and their family relationships.

MORE

• **Ask a coach or trainer to do some demonstrations of proper weight-training exercises and techniques. If he's a follower of Jesus, have that person share his story with your students.**
• **Show a YouTube video of The Power Team demonstrating the effects of their weight training (*www.thepowerteam.com*).**

1. What highs and lows come to mind when you think about the following things:

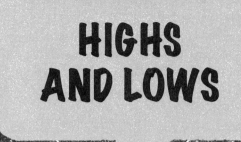

	HIGHS	LOWS
• Friendships:	_____	_____
• School:	_____	_____
• Family:	_____	_____
• Vacation:	_____	_____
• Food:	_____	_____
• Love:	_____	_____
• Sports:	_____	_____
• Achievements:	_____	_____
• Money:	_____	_____
• Dreams:	_____	_____

2. Check out Revelation 2:5. What does this verse have to do with "highs and lows"?

3. What's the high point in your life with God?

4. What's the low point in your life with God?

5. On a scale of 1 to 10 (with one being the lowest low and 10 being the highest high), at what elevation is your life with God today? Why?

6. What one thing do the following verses—Revelation 2:16, Revelation 2:22, Revelation 3:3, Revelation 3:19—have in common with Revelation 2:5?

7. What does it mean to repent?

8. How does repentance affect a person's elevation (high point or low point) with God?

9. What's one thing you need to repent of today?

THIS WEEK

Sometimes we feel as though life with God is a high point. Other times life with God feels like a low point. This discussion will help your students consider how repentance could be a key factor in moving them toward a high point with God.

OPENER

Take your group on a field trip to a higher elevation. If you live close to mountains or hills, assemble your group as high up as you can get them. If you live in an urban area, arrange for your group to meet at the top of the tallest building you can access. Ideally, you should gather in your regular meeting place to start with and then tell the group you're going on an adventure to an elevated place. After you arrive, tell them you're going to talk about highs and lows in life and you want them to experience this discussion from a "high point." Then move them into the first question on the TalkSheet.

THE DISCUSSION, BY NUMBERS

1. Have your group consider the 10 things listed in question one and write down their high point and low point in each category. After giving them a few minutes to consider their answers, allow your group to share what they wrote for each thing and why it was a high or low.

2. Now have your group read Revelation 2:5 and write how this verse relates to the discussion of highs and lows. Jesus is saying that our life with God can be measured in elevation. Sometimes followers of Jesus live the way God tells them to, resulting in a high point in their life with God. Other times, people live according to their own rules and they fall until they reach a low point in their life with God.

3. Have your group identify the high point in their life with God.

4. Now flip the question and have them name the low point in their life with God.

5. Ask your students to evaluate their current elevation by grading themselves on a scale of 1 to 10 (with 1 being the lowest low and 10 being the highest high)

regarding their life with God right now. Let them share their responses and why they chose that score.

6. Jesus calls for his followers who have fallen from a high point to *repent*. Give your group a chance to come to that conclusion. Then move on to question seven.

7. *Repent* means "to turn around and go in a different direction." In Greek, it's the word *metanoia* (pronounced met-uh-noy-uh), a military term. Picture a group of soldiers marching in one direction and then at the sound of their commander's charge, they turn and march in a different direction.

8. When we sin, we need to stop, turn around, and head in a new direction. Thus, sin leads us to a low point, while repentance changes our direction and gets us moving back toward a high point with God.

9. Let your group know they won't be sharing this answer, so encourage them to be honest. After you've given them time to write down their one thing, move on to The Close.

THE CLOSE

Have your group text or email you what they wrote for question nine as a form of accountability and a way for you to respond and pray for them in this step of repentance. Then leave them with Romans 8:38-39 as an encouragement about God's love for them. (For those who aren't yet followers of Jesus, the Bible clearly teaches that sin separates us from a relationship with God through Jesus.)

MORE
- **At the end of the discussion, invite those who haven't yet placed their faith, trust, and hope in Jesus for salvation and forgiveness of their sins to do it right then and mark that moment as their high point with God.**
- **As your group begins to gather, play the Steve Winwood song "Higher Love" to set the mood for the day. Email your group the iTunes link to the song later in the week as a reminder of the highs-and-lows discussion.**
- **Plan a trip or experience that will take your group to a new elevation—rock climbing, hiking, or even spelunking. Remember this principle: I heard and I forgot, I saw and I remembered, but I did it and I understood it.**

1. What words come to mind when you hear the word *faith*?

DEMONSTRATED FAITH

2. What's the difference between taking a step of faith and taking a chance on something that you want to happen?

3. What's the biggest step of faith you've seen one of your friends take?

4. What's the biggest step of faith you've seen your parents take?

5. What's the biggest step of faith you've taken in your life so far?

6. Check out Matthew 8:5-10 and write down what Jesus said about one person's faith.

7. Why do you think this person's demonstration of faith amazed Jesus?

8. If you could do one thing that would demonstrate your faith, what would you do?

9. This week Jesus would be amazed at my life of faith if I decided to…

THIS WEEK

Jesus declared that the centurion who believed Jesus could heal with just a word had more faith than anyone he'd met in Israel. Your group will discuss what faith is and what it might look like to have Jesus make a similar statement about their faith.

OPENER

Show the classic "leap of faith" scene from near the end of *Indiana Jones and the Last Crusade*. The clip shows Indiana (played by Harrison Ford) stepping off a cliff and onto an invisible bridge. After watching the clip, let your group know they'll be talking about what it means to live a life that demonstrates their faith, then head to the first question on the TalkSheet.

THE DISCUSSION, BY NUMBERS

1. Give your group a few moments to write down all the words and images that come to mind when they hear the word *faith*. Then take a few minutes and let them share.

2. This question is intended to get your students thinking. Don't worry about the correct answer. Just get them talking about the difference between taking a step of faith and taking a chance. Feel the freedom to leave it unresolved and let them know you'll come back to it in a bit (during The Close).

3. Have them take a few moments to write their answers to questions three, four, and five before discussing them with the group. Then have them reveal one of their friends' biggest steps of faith.

4. Move on and have them share about their parents' biggest step of faith.

5. Finally, have them talk about the biggest step of faith they've taken so far.

6. Now have them read Matthew 8:5-10, the story of the centurion who demonstrated a faith that amazed Jesus. Have someone read the passage aloud and then have the students write down what Jesus said.

7. Let your group members wrestle with this one. If they need some help, point them back to what the man said to Jesus in verses 8-9. Jesus offered to go to the man's house and heal his servant. However, because this man understood authority and power, he had complete confidence that all Jesus had to do was speak the word and his servant would be healed. Many people feel they must see to believe. But this man believed before seeing the results of his request. Point out that the verse says Jesus "was amazed." When the God of the universe is amazed by a person's faith, we should sit up and take notice.

8. Flip the conversation away from the story and back to the individuals in your group. Ask them to consider what they'd do if they could do anything in the world to demonstrate their faith. Let them ponder it for a moment before sharing their responses.

9. The goal for this question is to have your students consider what they might do that would amaze Jesus. Challenge them to take that step of faith and do it!

THE CLOSE

Read Hebrews 11:1, 6 aloud. Tell your students that taking a step of faith means you're moving toward what you truly believe God wants for your life. Your actions are backed by a certainty in the power and authority of Jesus to make it come to pass—if it's his will. Such faith dissolves fear and anxiety and allows us to live with a confidence that Jesus is pleased when we trust him and live our faith before him.

MORE

• Get your group together for a movie night and watch *Indiana Jones and the Last Crusade*. Go over the TalkSheet after the movie ends, but show the "leap of faith" scene one more time. As always, make sure any movie you watch with your students is appropriate for your group.

• Show your group the act of putting faith into action with a quick object lesson. You can have faith that a chair will hold you. However, your faith isn't really *faith* until you put all of your weight on the chair. So get a chair and take a seat. Simple, yet it makes the point.

• Let your group do a "faith exercise" together. Have your students take turns demonstrating their faith by falling backward into the arms of their friends. Have the rest of the group stand behind the falling individual and lock arms to make the catch. The person who falls will show her faith by being certain that her friends will actually catch her.

1. Who's the most honored or decorated person you know?

2. What's the greatest honor or award you've ever received?

3. What would be the ultimate honor or award you could ever receive?

4. What's the one righteous thing you've done or achieved in your life that nobody really knows about, but you'd probably get some kind of medal or award for if the world did know about it?

5. Check out Isaiah 64:6 and write down what God says about our righteous acts.

6. What can we learn about God from the song "Jesus Loves Me"?

7. Where does the Bible "tell us so"?

MEDAL OF HONOR

THIS WEEK

This TalkSheet will help your group understand that God loves us for free, rather than for what we do. In fact God says all of our righteous activity is like a bunch of filthy rags. So unless God loves us for something besides what we do, we're all in deep weeds!

OPENER

Ask a decorated war veteran to share the stories behind his various medals. If you can find someone who received the Medal of Honor, that would be ideal. It may be best to do this in an interview style so you can keep the pace moving along. Thank the person for sharing before you move on to the TalkSheet questions.

THE DISCUSSION, BY NUMBERS

1. Get your group talking about people they know who've received awards, honors, or medals. These honors could be athletic, scholastic, civic, or anything in the vein of being recognized for what the person has done.

2. Now have them consider their own lives and discuss what they consider to be their greatest honor or award so far.

3. Challenge your group to dream a bit. Have them think about the greatest honor or award they could ever achieve in their lifetime. Then let them share their ideas with the group.

4. Ask your students to talk about one great thing they've done that nobody really knows about. You might even want to use the word "righteous" to describe what they've done (just to introduce the term before it shows up in the next discussion question).

5. Now have your group look up Isaiah 64:6 and write down God's description of our righteous acts: A bunch of filthy rags. (Actually, that's the sanitized version of what the term really means!) Make sure your group understands that what God is saying is that nothing we do compares with his mercy, love, and righteousness. In other words, if God loves us, then it won't be due to anything we've done to impress God.

6. Help your group recall the words to "Jesus Loves Me" and have them write down what they can learn about God in the lyrics:

   Jesus loves me this I know.
   For the Bible tells me so.

Little ones to him belong.
They are weak, but he is strong.
Yes, Jesus loves me.
Yes, Jesus loves me.
Yes, Jesus loves me.
The Bible tells me so.

7. Have your group members talk about where the Bible "tells them so" concerning Jesus' love for them. Allow your group to give whatever answers they come up with before moving on to The Close.

THE CLOSE

Walk your group through "The Roman Road," which gives some starting points in looking at God's love for people. Have your students look up the following verses with you:

- Romans 3:23—Everyone sins.
- Romans 6:23—The price for sin is death, but salvation through Jesus is free.
- Romans 5:8—God demonstrates his love for people as Christ died in our place.
- Romans 10:9-10, 13—All can be saved and made right with God through Jesus.

After walking your group through what the Bible says about the love of God in these passages in Romans, invite anyone in your group who'd like to begin a relationship with Jesus to do so at this time. Close your time by leading your group in prayer. Be sure and make the point that nothing we do can earn God's love. It's only through the free gift of God through his Son Jesus' death on the cross that people can be made righteous before God.

MORE

• **You may want to record the stories of individuals talking about their military awards and honors, rather than have a live interview, just so you can control the time.**

• **Approach the interview with a decorated war veteran as an opportunity to pray for our country and those serving and protecting the freedoms we enjoy as a result of their sacrifice.**

• **If the local high school or middle school has an awards display case, get permission to lead your discussion in front of that trophy case to help drive home the point of the lesson. If you do this, instead of having an interview with a decorated military person, see if you can get a coach to talk about some of the great teams or athletes who won the awards displayed in the case.**

1. Make a list of all the chores you're responsible for doing each week.

2. Which chores do you enjoy doing the most? Which chores do you enjoy doing the least?

3. What's the one thing you're most likely to procrastinate doing?

4. Check out Philippians 1:6 and write down what God is responsible for completing in life.

5. Do you feel like God is keeping this promise in Philippians 1:6 or procrastinating the work he's supposed to be doing in your life?

6. What's an area of your life in which you believe God—

   • Is about finished

   • Is still working on it

   • Has a long way to go

   • Hasn't even started

   • Needs to start

7. Check out what 2 Peter 3:8-9 says about God's view of time and the timing of God's promise and write what it says in your own words.

8. One thing that will look different about my life when God has completed his work in me is…

9. When it comes to my life with God, one place in which I've been procrastinating is…

THIS WEEK

This TalkSheet compares the work we're responsible for completing with a specific work that God has promised to complete. Is God a procrastinator, or is his timing just different than ours?

OPENER

Start with a friendly competition between two students to see who can make the neatest bed in one minute. For this competition you'll need two beds (mattresses or cots will do), two sets of sheets, two blankets, two bedspreads, and two pillows. Fold all of the bed linens so it takes a little time for the contestants to unfold the items and make the beds "from scratch." The maker of the most completely made (and neat) bed at the end of one minute is declared the winner. After the contest remind your group that almost everybody is responsible for completing things in their lives. At this point have your group look at question one on the TalkSheet.

THE DISCUSSION, BY NUMBERS

1. Have your students think about all of the chores they're responsible for completing each week. These jobs can include work assigned at home, at school, and with their various extracurricular activities or teams. Have them list as many chores as they can and then take a few minutes to allow your group to talk through a portion of their lists.

2. Have them answer questions two and three before going through them with your group. Simply ask them to review their list in question one and select those items they enjoy doing the most and the least for question two.

3. Have them select from their list in question one the item they're most likely to procrastinate doing each week. After they have questions two and three completed, let each student share their answers to both at one time, rather than going around the group twice.

4. It says in the Bible that God is also responsible for completing some work. Have your group turn to Philippians 1:6 and read the verse. Then have them write down what that verse is saying to them regarding the work God is responsible for completing in their lives.

5. This question is intended to get them talking more about the verse they just read. Let them discuss whether or not God has been procrastinating about doing the work in their lives. Make sure they give a bit of reasoning.

6. Now ask your group to complete the following sentences with examples from their lives. God—
   - Is about finished
   - Is still working on it
   - Has a long way to go
   - Hasn't even started
   - Needs to start

7. Ask your group to look up 2 Peter 3:8-9 and write in their own words what these verses say about God's view of time and how it relates to what he's promised to do. Basically, God views time in a more holistic manner than we do. It also assures us that God will do what he's promised in his timing and not before.

8. Have your students complete the sentence with a word or phrase that fits their life, and then let them share it with the group.

9. As they wrap up this discussion, challenge them to be honest on this question. Have them complete this final sentence with a word that best fits their life situation. Then have them share what they wrote with the group.

THE CLOSE

Challenge your group to make their beds each morning without procrastinating and with great care and deliberate focus. Ask them to consider making their beds as part of their prayer time and to begin their day talking with God and asking him to help them be faithful and quick to respond to any opportunities to make Christ known in their lives today. Tell them: "Delayed obedience is disobedience."

MORE

- **Put your group on the "bell-prayer schedule" (described in session 42). Challenge them to be mindful of God's perfect timing by committing to whisper a prayer each time they hear a bell ring. They might be amazed at how a 10-second whispered prayer can change their perspective for the next hour.**
- **Review Ecclesiastes 3 with your group to enhance their perspectives on what God says about issues of timing.**
- **Process with your group how a verse like Ephesians 2:10 might play out in their lives when it comes to "God's work." What might some of those "good works" be? If we know what they are and don't do them, then are we being disobedient or just procrastinating?**

1. One item that I've never been able to get rid of or sell is…

Because…

EAST AND WEST

2. Have you ever retrieved something of yours from the trash or donation pile that your parents were trying to get rid of?

3. Check out what 1 John 1:8-9 says and write down what you think it means.

4. Now look at what Psalm 103:11-13 says. What does God do with our transgressions (sins)?

5. What's the meaning of the expression "as far as the east is from the west"? How far is that?

6. Why would God do this to our sin once he's forgiven it?

7. Why do people hang on to their sin instead of letting God remove all traces of it from their lives?

THIS WEEK

Sometimes we allow our past sins to affect our present, even though God has forgiven us. This TalkSheet will help your students leave their forgiven sins in the past, just like God does.

OPENER

Start by showing your students an old keepsake or toy that you haven't been able to let go. Give a bit of history as to why you feel so sentimental about it and why you've chosen to hang on to it over the years. After telling your stories, have your group focus on the TalkSheet questions to continue the discussion.

THE DISCUSSION, BY NUMBERS

1. Let your group join the conversation by identifying one item they've held on to and why they haven't been able to throw it away or donate it.

2. Talk about how parents get on "spring cleaning" kicks. Ask your students to share about a time when their parents tried to throw something away without their consent, but they retrieved it from the trash. Why was the rescued item so important to them?

3. Make the point that although we all have possessions we've hung on to for too long, we probably have things on the inside of our lives that need to be dealt with and discarded as well. It may be a known sin or a secret one. Have your group look up 1 John 1:8-9 and write down what it means. The best response is to confess our sins to Jesus (and whomever we've wronged) and allow him to forgive us and make us right with him again.

4. Now have your group read Psalm 103:11-13 and write what God does with our sins (transgressions). This verse says that because God loves us, he removes our sins from us as far as the east is from the west.

5. This was a phrase used in biblical days to describe a separation of great distance. Such separation could literally mean for eternity and never to return.

6. Give your group time to process this question. It's okay if they don't fully understand it. Just make sure they know that God wants us to move forward in our lives with Jesus, not stay in bondage to our past. And while God wants us to learn from our mistakes and sins, many people keep asking for forgiveness from the same sins that Jesus has already forgiven.

7. We must learn to take God at his word and move forward in light of this truth—God has forgiven our sin and removed it from us. Too often, Christians listen to the lies of the enemy instead of standing on the truth of God's Word. If Satan can distract us with the past, then he's immobilized us even if he no longer owns our hearts.

THE CLOSE

You'll need to have a small rock for each person in your group. You'll also need a couple of Sharpie pens. Give your students time to select a rock from the pile. Then ask them to focus on one sin that's still impacting them and deal with it before God. If they need to confess a sin, encourage them to do so. If it's an issue they've already dealt with but never moved past, then point out that sometimes intentionally doing something to mark a change can help them move forward. Ask the students to write a word on their rocks that represents their sin. Then challenge them to throw the rock as far as they can (see the More section for some ideas) as a way to remind themselves of what God has already done. Give your group as much time as they need and then close in prayer.

MORE

• **This is a great TalkSheet to do during an outing to the beach or a lake so the students can throw their rocks into a body of water at the end. Sometimes meeting in a different environment will stimulate honest discussion about difficult issues.**

• **If you don't have access to a body of water, have your group throw their rocks into a field, over a cliff, or onto a garbage dump. Just give them a chance to rear back and chunk their rocks as far as they can.**

• **If you're meeting by a body of water with some rocks or stones on the shore, have a rock-skipping contest. See whose rock bounces the most before it sinks.**

1. **If you received an invisibility cloak as a Christmas present, how or when would you have used it this week?**

THE CLOAK

2. **If you had the choice to change the power of the cloak from making you invisible to giving you another special ability, what would you choose?**

3. **Check out the following passages and write down the attribute that's found in all of them:**

   • Philippians 4:10-13

   • 1 Timothy 6:6-8

   • Hebrews 13:5

4. **What do you think it means for a person to be content?**

5. **Why do you think God wants us to be content in our lives?**

6. **The area of my life in which I'm most content would have to be…**

7. **The area of my life in which I need God's help to become content is…**

8. **How would becoming more content change the way you experience life?**

THIS WEEK

This TalkSheet will show your group what God has to say about being content. Contentment is an attribute that's highly valued in God's economy. What would life be like if we learned to be content, rather than always wanting more?

OPENER

Start by showing or describing one of the greatest Christmas presents you ever received. Then have your students talk about theirs. After getting everyone involved, ask your group if they remember Harry Potter's most treasured Christmas present. If you have any Harry Potter fans in your group, they should know that Dumbledore gave Harry an invisibility cloak during his first Christmas at Hogwarts. If they're unaware of how the cloak works, tell them it allows the person who's under it to become invisible. (If you want to show a clip from the movie, see the More section below.)

THE DISCUSSION, BY NUMBERS

1. Let your group run with this question a bit to see how they would've used the invisibility cloak. You may just get some insight into what's going on in the lives of some of your students. After they've all had a chance to answer, move on to the next question.
2. Discuss what attribute your students would like the cloak to give them, if they had the choice, such as superior strength, being able to fly, turning to vapor, and so on. Encourage them to be creative with their answers. Just make sure they also give the reason behind it.
3. All three passages refer to the attribute of being content regardless of the situation.
4. Now ask your group to talk about what it means for a person to be content. Let them wrestle with the concept a bit before giving them the answer. In part, being content means being thankful for the things you have and being at peace with the place or season of life you're experiencing, regardless of the situation. People who experience this type of contentment find their identity, security, provision, and joy in the person of Jesus. Another part of being content is not constantly wanting more, more, more.

5. Ask your group to talk about why God believes it's important for us to be content. Let them wrestle with this question and concept before giving them an answer.
6. Now ask them to consider the area of their life in which they feel the most content. You may need to give them a couple of examples, such as relationships, schoolwork, and security at home. But don't offer the examples too quickly. See what they come up with first.
7. Challenge your group to be honest and think deeply on this question. Let them share their answers and thank them for being vulnerable about the area in which they need God's help in the days ahead.
8. What benefit might be gained if your students were to become more content with who and where they are in life? Allow your group some time to answer this question.

THE CLOSE

One way to become more content is to focus on being more thankful. Challenge your group to list all of their blessings on the backside of their TalkSheets. Then encourage them to fast from asking God for more this week. Close your time by thanking God for all that you've already received.

MORE

• Show a scene from one of the Harry Potter movies that shows Harry using the invisibility cloak. In *Harry Potter and the Sorcerer's Stone*, Harry receives the invisibility cloak as a Christmas present in scene 21. The following scene, number 22, shows Harry using the invisibility cloak in the library and walking down the hallway. As always, be sure to preview any movie clips to make sure they're appropriate for your group.

• Give each student a small, wrapped Christmas present with nothing inside the box. (Tell them there's nothing in the box so they don't open it.) The present should serve as a reminder that God wants us to be content with whatever we have or don't have, regardless of our situation.

1. What was the winning team's main strategy for creating a structure that was not only the tallest, but also held together?

HOLDING IT TOGETHER

2. List three areas of your life that seem to be standing tall and holding together.

3. List three areas of your life that seem to be falling apart instead of standing tall.

4. What's the main reason why these things in your life (see question two) seem to be holding together?

5. What's the main reason why things in your life (see question three) seem to be falling apart?

6. Check out what the apostle Paul said in Colossians 1:17 and write it down.

7. What do you think that verse means as it relates to your life?

8. The thing I really need Jesus to hold together in my life is…

THIS WEEK

This TalkSheet will guide your group in considering the apostle Paul's statement about how Jesus holds all things together. Through a variety of object lessons, they'll explore what seems to be holding together and what seems to be falling apart in their lives.

OPENER

Start with a friendly competition to see who can figure out the best and most effective ways to "hold it together." After dividing your group into teams of four to six people, give each team a box of spaghetti, a package of large marshmallows, and a box of Froot Loops cereal. The object is to see which team can create the tallest freestanding structure in 10 minutes. After time is up, declare the team with the tallest object the winner. Then have your group take a look at the first question on the TalkSheet.

THE DISCUSSION, BY NUMBERS

1. Let your group examine the winning structure and write down their guess as to the team's strategy for making it both tall and stable (i.e., hold together). Then let your group members discuss their ideas.
2. Help your students make a mental shift from constructing objects out of marshmallows, spaghetti, and Froot Loops, to thinking about their own lives. Ask them to consider what things seem to be "standing tall and holding together" and what things seem to be "falling apart" in their lives today. You may want to offer an example of each to set the tone of the discussion. Have them answer questions two through five before sharing their answers.
3. See question two.
4. See question two.
5. See question two.
6. Now have your group look up Colossians 1:15-17. Let them know that God inspired and preserved these words, and they may provide a new perspective in the conversation today. Have them write verse 17 in the space provided: "He

[Jesus] is before all things, and in him all things hold together."
7. Ask your students to write what they think that verse means in their own lives. Then allow them to share their answers with the group.
8. Finish the discussion by asking your students to finish the sentence: "The thing I really need Jesus to hold together in my life is _____." Give them some time to consider their response, then go around the group and let each person share what they wrote.

THE CLOSE

Wrap up by asking your group to "hold together" by standing in a circle and linking arms. Pray about your students' responses to question eight. Ask Jesus to hold them together in their lives and pray that Jesus would give each person the courage to trust him and the faith to keep walking forward in relationship with him and with others who are following him.

MORE
• **If you have a large group, start by dividing them into larger teams of 10 to 12 people and let them see who can build—and hold together—the tallest human pyramid. The winner will be the team that utilizes all of its members, builds the highest structure in two minutes' time, and holds it together without falling.**
• **Start by having your students pair off. Then give each team a dollar's worth of pennies (100) and a roll of duct tape. See which team can construct the tallest and most stable structure of pennies in 10 minutes. To make it even more interesting, increase the amount of pennies to five dollars' worth (500).**
• **Start by dividing your group into teams of three and give each a deck of playing cards and a glue stick. Have the teams work together for 10 or 15 minutes to see which one can build the highest house of cards. If you really want to make it challenging, don't give them a glue stick! The team with the highest house of cards that remains standing at the end of the time limit is the winner.**